OF
UNIVE

A Student's Guide to Living and Studying Away From Home

I just brought a few friends round for tea Mum— hope you don't mind...

For Richard and Gus

About the author

Sally Alger graduated from University College London with a BSc Honours Degree in Anthropology after three impoverished but happy years. After graduating she worked briefly in a museum and in advertising, before going into journalism. She contributes regularly to magazines and newspapers and has edited an award-winning magazine for students.

OFF TO UNIVERSITY?

A Student's Guide to Living and Studying Away From Home

Sally Alger

DP Publications Ltd
Aldine Place
London W12 8AW
1993

ACKNOWLEDGEMENTS

My thanks to all the students who have contributed
their thoughts, experiences, advice and helpful
suggestions during the preparation of this book.

A CIP Catalogue record for this book is available
from the British Library

ISBN 0 85805 067 7
Copyright Sally Alger © 1993

First edition 1993

Printed in Great Britain by
The Guernsey Press Company,
Guernsey, Channel Islands

Pageset by DP Publications
Book illustrations by Cath Chadwick

INTRODUCTION

Leaving home to go to university is a major event in anybody's life. And the big question you're undoubtedly asking yourself is: what *is* life at university going to be like?

That's the question many students still find themselves asking the day they arrive at college, and often right through to the end of Freshers Week. Some colleges and student unions are pretty good at giving their new students an idea of what to expect, over and above the basic information provided in the official prospectus. However, far too many new students are left floundering in the deep end, with very little practical advice and information to help them through the confusing first days. All this at a time when they have just left home, are living in a strange town and without the proverbial shoulder to cry on.

Of course, the majority of new students manage to find their feet by the end of the first two or three weeks, with or without the help of the college authorities. There's something about the camaraderie of all being new boys and girls together that tends to speed up the whole process. But for some students, being confronted with so many first time experiences can sour the first term, and sometimes cast a longer shadow over what should be the happiest and most carefree period of their lives.

However much you look forward to the challenges and freedom that your newly independent lifestyle promises, don't be surprised if you feel a little apprehensive too – and even a twinge of regret at all you're leaving behind. You'll be saying good-bye to a familiar and comfortable way of life, and all sorts of things you could happily take for granted: family, friends, teachers, school, regular meals, a constant supply of food in the fridge and toilet rolls in the loo, free central heating and so on.

You'll be aware, too, that far from the popular image of student life being one long party, there are increasing pressures on students today. Lack of money (which isn't new) and far fewer chances to earn it, a greater stress on studying to achieve a worthwhile, job-earning degree (but with no guarantee of any sort of job at the end of it all), poor and overpriced accommodation, increasingly crowded lecture rooms and fewer study resources.

And if that's not enough to be coping with, another pressure has been added to the student lot: debt. It's current government policy to 'encourage' students and their families to invest in their own education. Consequently parents now find themselves having to make up their offspring's grants (or not, as the case may be) at a time when they can ill afford to do so, given the recessionary times. And the vast majority of students have to take out government-backed loans and interest-laden bank overdrafts – just to make ends meet. All of this has to be paid back – and a time when a new graduate, embarking on the first, ill-paid rungs of his or her career, could do without the additional burden of debt.

So why bother going to university at all, if you're committing yourself to three years of dire penury? It's true that some people are asking themselves this question, but for most students it doesn't even begin to arise. You are going to university because you want to widen your horizons and become independent. You want to spend three years or so studying a subject that intrigues you, and may even lead you on to a worthwhile career. You want to meet new people and avail yourself of all sorts of opportunities and experiences that you would never have in a lifetime of staying at home. But most of all you want to have a good time.

Independence brings with it responsibilities. As well as getting to grips with a new course, you have to take charge of all other aspects of your life, perhaps for the first time. You'll have to organise and juggle your finances and also learn the practicalities of running your own household, from dealing with a landlord, to paying bills and shopping and cooking for yourself. There's no great mystery to all of this – but it can seem complex if you've never had to handle such things before.

That's where *Off To University?* comes in. The intention of the book is not only to help you get the most out of your time at university, but to fill in all those frustrating information gaps. So when you do arrive at college, you'll feel confident and in control, equipped to enjoy the heady pleasures of Freshers Week and the terms that follow. It's a comprehensive, no-nonsense, warts-and-all guide to life at college. Within its pages you should find an answer to all your questions, worries and conundrums. If you don't, please write and let me know. It would be nice to think that a new generation of students can benefit from your experiences, in the way that I hope you will benefit from the students whose experiences have contributed to this present edition.

Sally Alger
July 1993

CONTENTS

Contents

Chapter 1

GETTING THERE

Choosing the right course – the application procedure – applying for a grant – what to expect at interviews and open days – what to do if you haven't got your grades – the Clearing process – why trying again next year could be a good idea – organising your move to college

Most people look back on their years at university with a warm glow, fondly remembering the freedom and total lack of responsibility, the luxurious lie-ins before a midday lecture, the long nights passed putting the world to rights over cheap wine, the even longer summer vacations spent back-packing in some exotic location. The poverty, the damp, cramped and overpriced accommodation, the stomach-knotting pressure of working through the night before a crucial exam. Yes, one day you too will have all that to look back on.

But first, you've got to get there.

CHOOSING THE RIGHT COURSE

A major factor in how much you enjoy your time at college is going to be your choice of course. If you've chosen well, you'll find it stimulating and demanding in the proper sense of stretching your mind and your capacity to think, analyse and communicate ideas. If you haven't chosen well, you're more likely to feel dissatisfied, bored and possibly out of your depth.

So how do you make sure that you choose well? Having a good idea of what subject you want to study is a start. Equally important is understanding why you want to study it. Are you choosing that subject because:

(a) It's your best or favourite A Level subject?

(b) It should improve your chances of landing a good job when you graduate?

(c) You have a very real interest in the subject and want the opportunity to explore it in much greater depth?

(d) You already have a vocation, maybe law, in mind?

(e) You don't really know what you want to study but your parents and teachers are pressuring you to apply for a place at university and have suggested the subject?

When you analyse the above reasons, it's pretty obvious that (b), (c) and (d) are more likely to lead to an enjoyable and fulfilling three years or so at university and a more successful choice of degree course, not least because if your studies do go through a sticky patch you've got the motivation to persevere. Whereas reason (e) is virtually doomed to failure because you're letting others decide for you without any real consideration of your own interests, ambitions and ability. If reason (e) – and maybe even (a) – have a ring of truth about them, it might be more sensible to give yourself a breathing space and put off going to university for a year or so, until you have a firmer idea of what you want to do.

Going about choosing a course and college

Once you've decided that you do want to go to university, and you know what subject you want to study, you can set about choosing a course and drawing up a shortlist of potential colleges. This requires a good deal of research on your part, because you're limited in the number of courses/colleges you can apply for (eight). To be able to make a choice you'll need information and advice.

Getting hold of information is easy enough; advice you have to be a bit more selective about. You'll have no shortage of people eager to give their penny's worth, especially when it comes to recommending their *alma mater*. The chances are, though, that however well meant their advice is, it's probably out of date by a couple of decades – especially if it comes from teachers and parents. On the other hand, if you have the opportunity to speak to a recent old boy or girl from your school or college who's currently studying at a college on your provisional list you'll get a more accurate idea of what the place is really like, warts and all.

Both your school and your local library will have the latest reference and handbooks detailing the courses available for the coming academic year and the qualification requirements. Use these to make a comprehensive list of all the colleges in the UK offering the course you're looking for, and then write or telephone for a prospectus from each one. A prospectus will itemise the range of courses available at a particular institution in some detail, but it will also give useful information concerning the facilities available for students (libraries, language laboratories, halls of residence etc), the physical character of the campus (eg city-centre or park-like surroundings on the edge of town), plus a general impression of the town or city itself. Thus, depending on whether you feel you'd be happier in a city or a more rural setting, you can use this information to help narrow down your possible options.

Although the decision of which courses and colleges to apply for must in the end rest with you, your careers teacher or Local Education Authority (LEA) careers adviser will be happy to talk through the pros and cons to help you get the options clear in your own mind.

Putting in your application

Your school or LEA will provide you with an application form and the current handbook which lists all the course options available at universities throughout the UK.

From 1st September 1993 the Universities Central Council of Admissions (UCCA) and the Polytechnics Central Admissions System (PCAS) unite under one organisation: the Universities and Colleges Admissions Service (UCAS). You can contact UCAS direct (for information or an application form) by writing to PO Box 28, Cheltenham, Glos GL50 3SA (telephone 0242-222444).

Your application form has a great deal hanging on it – possibly even your future. Right now, though, it has to attract the attention and interest of the colleges listed on it. So if you need any help or advice on filling it in, do ask for help.

Before putting pen to paper (black ink, as it's going to be photocopied and distributed to the listed colleges) practise writing your answers first on a separate sheet of paper or on a photocopy. The form itself should be clean (no coffee or food stains) and completed in legible handwriting (if yours isn't great

Interests:
watching TV, sleeping, drinking beer
Visual arts, meditation, research
for my definitive opus on the
History of Brewing.

either print your answers or get someone else to fill it in for you). Make sure that the course/college reference numbers are accurate, and that you provide all the information asked for. When you've finished, pass it on to your referee to add his or her personal recommendation. (Keep a copy for yourself, so you remember what information you gave.) Remember to send the form by the deadline (the middle of October if you've included Oxford or Cambridge, otherwise the middle of December), or your efforts will have been for nothing.

One thing you should get advice on from your careers teacher or the LEA careers officer is the order in which you list your colleges on the application form. Rightly or wrongly, some universities get very sniffy if they are placed towards the bottom. You can safely forget getting any sort of offer, for example, from either Oxford or Cambridge if you put them anywhere other than first.

Receiving offers

You should start getting offers early in spring. If you are really fortunate you'll get an *unconditional offer*, which means the you've already satisfied the college's requirements for admission and they can't wait to get you on board. However, you are more likely to receive a *conditional offer*, which means the place is yours provided you achieve the A Level grades the college asks for. If you don't get any offers, all is not lost as you have another chance to obtain a place in August, once the A Level results are out and it's known how many empty places remain to be filled.

APPLYING FOR A GRANT

You may be eligible for a full or partial grant to help support you financially through your degree course. Apply as early as possible in the year you are intending to go to college, regardless of whether you have a firm offer of a place or not. The process can take some time, mostly because hard-pressed local authorities don't put students at the top of their list of priorities. Leaving it late can also mean that your grant cheque won't be waiting ready for you when you arrive at college in the autumn.

You can obtain the relevant forms from your school, or you can contact your LEA direct. First you'll receive an *application form*, which the LEA will use to decide if you are eligible for a grant.

If you are, you'll then receive a *grant assessment form*, which will decide how much grant you get. Your parents (or spouse, if you have one) will have to complete a financial statement regarding all sources of their income, and this will be taken into account when your grant is assessed. If they refuse to provide the necessary information (which they have every right to do) you won't be awarded a grant.

You will also receive a *college acceptance form*, which you should send to your college as soon as you have a place confirmed on a course (if you have a conditional offer this may be in August, when you receive your A Level results). Once this has been completed and returned to your LEA, the latter will agree to pay your tuition fees (direct to the college) and your grant (in the form of a termly cheque, which you collect at college). You'll receive an *award letter* in official confirmation, which you should take with you to college to show when you pick up your grant cheque.

Although your grant is awarded for the full length of your course, the amount will be reviewed annually and reflect any changes in your or your parents' financial circumstances.

Your grant isn't intended to cover all your living expenses, even if you get the full amount. You will be expected to supplement your income with a Student Loan and if necessary – as is highly likely – your own part-time and vacation earnings.

Chapter 5, 'Maximising Your Income', gives more information about the various conditions which apply to your eligibility for a grant, plus the additional allowances that are available under special circumstances.

WHAT TO EXPECT AT INTERVIEWS AND OPEN DAYS

Your environment is just as important as your course. You're going to have to spend at least three years there, after all. Most universities hold special open days for prospective students, and they are an excellent opportunity to get the feel of the place before you finally commit yourself to studying there. The one drawback is that the travel costs can be high, depending on the distances of the institutions from your own home.

Open days are usually informal events, during the course of which you'll be introduced to the department staff and given a conducted tour around the campus. With any luck you'll also meet some second or third years students, giving you the opportunity to ask some pertinent questions and get some honest answers in return! If possible, try to allow yourself enough time to have a quick look around the town or city.

Interviews

The point of an interview is for a college to get an idea of the kind of person you are, and whether you'd fit in, contribute to and benefit from life at university. It's your big opportunity to sell yourself. Make an impression on the interviewer and he or she may be prepared to overlook slightly dodgy grades when you finally get your results.

You don't have to demonstrate an in-depth knowledge and understanding of the subject you're hoping to study. However, you will be expected to demonstrate some enthusiasm and special interest in it, to the extent of having done some of your own private reading around it. If you're applying for a 'creative' course (eg art or architecture) you'll be asked to bring along a portfolio of work. For a language course you can expect to have to converse in the appropriate language. If you want to study a subject with a strong vocational element (teaching, social work, medicine, law) you'll be expected to demonstrate a certain level of personal commitment.

❏ Students often agonise over what to wear to an interview, and parents and teachers usually give inappropriate advice, partly because things have changed since their days at college. It's not like a job interview, where appearances can count for a great deal. But you should feel comfortable and confident. Turning up in a formal suit when your interviewer and everyone else on the campus is in jeans can send your confidence diving. Smartish, clean casual clothes are usually fine. The only exceptions might be for the

more formal disciplines such as law and medicine. If in doubt, play it safe and call the department for their thoughts on the matter.

❏ You can be reasonably sure of being asked certain standard questions, giving you an opportunity to practise answers beforehand. For example: Why do you want to study that subject? Why at that college? Why did you choose your specific A Level subjects? What do you like doing in your spare time? Have you done any of your own reading around the subject?

❏ It won't impress your interviewer if you are vague about the actual course you're hoping to spend three years studying. Make sure you've read thoroughly the description in the prospectus, and feel free to ask questions about the course, the way the department is run, and what life at the college is like in general.

WHAT HAPPENS IF YOU DON'T ACHIEVE THE A LEVEL GRADES YOU'D HOPED FOR?

It's disappointing, especially after all your hard work and sacrifices. But it's not the end of the world – you have several options, and that includes still getting to college this autumn.

It's important to be home near the telephone the day you get your results so that you can act quickly to find an alternative course if necessary. Other students equally eager to find a place will be doing the same. However, do try and resist the temptation to accept any old course simply to get to university. You may be better off and happier in the long run if you take your time to find something more suitable, even if that means applying again next year.

You could still get on your chosen course

If you've only just missed the grades asked for by your prospective college it's worth telephoning the admissions tutor immediately and explaining your position. It's likely that other applicants for your course have also missed their grades. Exam results aren't the only deciding factor as to whether a person will make a good student or not, and if you sound determined and committed you could impress the admissions tutor enough to offer you the place anyway.

Did you include an 'insurance' choice on your original application?

When considering which colleges to put on their application forms many students include a course that requires lower grades as a kind of insurance policy. If you have received a conditional offer from your insurance choice and you have met the grades, your place will automatically be confirmed.

Going through the Clearing process

Despite the fierce competition for places, there will be many that are still empty in August and September, either because applicants haven't met the terms of their conditional offers or students who have had a place confirmed have decided to defer theirs for a year. So the instant the A Level results are out, the Clearing system swings into action to fill those places.

You have an excellent chance of getting a place through Clearing – one in ten students get theirs this way – though you may have to be a bit flexible about the actual course or its content, and also the location. You will automatically be sent a Clearing form if your conditional place hasn't been confirmed.

Using your own initiative

If you're determined to get to college this autumn don't waste time waiting for your Clearing form to arrive. You can contact colleges direct yourself to find out if there's a vacancy on a suitable course. Throughout late summer the quality daily and Sunday newspapers publish full lists of course vacancies. You can use these to research and draw up a shortlist of possible courses (your local library has copies daily). Telephone the course admissions tutor yourself (colleges aren't impressed when a parent calls). Try to sound enthusiastic and positive, and if you feel nervous, have some notes to hand which cover the main points you want to get across. You have a big advantage in that you already know your grades, and if you sound like the sort of student the college is looking for, you could be offered a place there and then.

TRYING AGAIN NEXT YEAR

Rather than rush into a decision – and a course – that you end up regretting, you'd be far better off forgetting university for this autumn and trying again for next year. This would give you a much-appreciated break from the education conveyor belt, and even more important, a valuable breathing space to consider more carefully what you really want to study, and maybe even what you want to do career-wise. In all the rush to send off your applications, not to mention the pressure of studying for your A Levels, you may not have given it quite the consideration such a far-reaching decision requires. And if you're not really sure what you want to do, then a year off to think about it is essential.

Use that year constructively, both in your own interests and because a prospective university will want to be reassured that you've spent the time doing something enterprising or socially useful, rather than mooching around at home. Chapter 9, 'Taking A Year Off', offers useful suggestions, plus practical advice on how to get the plans for your year's break off the ground.

Resitting your A Levels

If your A Level grades really weren't that great and could handicap your chances of obtaining a place next year, you should consider resitting them in November or January, depending on when your examinations board schedules retakes. Your school will be happy to make the necessary arrangements, including organising any essays and tutorials that might benefit you. You won't have to return to school full time. In the meantime you can reapply for another place, find a part-time job and plan how you're going to spend the rest of the year off. And because you'll know the results of your retakes quite quickly (ie several months before students who are sitting their exams in the summer), any place you are offered will be confirmed that much sooner.

Putting off university for longer

You don't have to go to university straight from school. More and more people are taking time out of education to work, raise families, travel the world and so on, returning to full-time higher education sometimes years later.

The advantages of deferring a university degree course are many, but perhaps the most important is that when you do decide to pick up your education, you're more likely to be a better motivated, more committed student, and as someone who's experienced life in the real world, you'll have a great deal to contribute on your own account to college life. This is precisely why the majority of education establishments go out of their way to encourage so-called 'mature' students, even to the extent of making the application procedure more flexible.

When you are ready to apply again, your local LEA careers service will be able to advise you on the procedure, or you can write direct to UCAS for information and an application form (see above for the address). It's also worth contacting the admissions tutor of your shortlisted colleges direct, as you may be able to bypass the usual applications procedure.

ORGANISING YOUR MOVE TO UNIVERSITY

By the time you get your exam results and your place confirmed, you don't have much time to get yourself organised for your departure – even less if you got a place at the last minute through Clearing. Other chapters in the book cover in detail many of the areas on the following checklist.

❑ Find somewhere to live with the assistance of your college accommodation office.

❑ Ensure that your application for a grant has been sent to your LEA and is proceeding without any problems (you should receive a letter from them confirming the award).

❑ Get details of the course contents, plus a summer reading list.

❑ Get your personal finances organised. Open a student bank or building society account, draw up a budget plan, make sure you have enough money to tide you over for the first couple of weeks in case your grant cheque is delayed.

❑ Get together important documents and information that you'll require for registration etc: your LEA award letter, birth/adoption certificate, a dozen passport photographs, NHS/medical card.

❑ Buy cut-price stationery in the 'back to school' promotions.

□ Start collecting crockery and kitchen utensils, especially if you're in self-catering accommodation.

□ Sort out the clothes you'll be taking, including buying any essentials while you can still afford them. Remember to check out local charity shops regularly.

□ Make sure you've got your friends' new college addresses.

□ Make a list of the personal things you'll be taking with you to college: a few favourite books and music cassettes or CDs; posters/pictures; a radio, TV, stereo system; a hairdryer; a word processor or personal computer; bicycle; bedlinen, towels and perhaps a brightly coloured or ethnic bedspread to make your room more homely; your teddy bear (you'd be surprised how many students do!); toiletries.

□ Find out if your parents' house contents insurance policy covers you for the above; if not, arrange a policy.

□ Buy a trunk so you can send some of your possessions on in advance.

□ If you're going to be sharing a flat, arrange for gas and electricity to be connected ready for your arrival.

□ Decide which day you want to move into your hall of residence or flat and work out the travel arrangements; organise a lift, book a train or coach seat (services are usually very busy that particular weekend); send your trunk a few days before by Red Star.

□ Organise a farewell dinner with your family!

Chapter 2

FINDING SOMEWHERE TO LIVE

Applying for accommodation – pros and cons of living in hall – living in a flat or lodgings – finding your own place to live – safety and security precautions – lodgings – when you find somewhere to live – tenancy agreements – problems with your landlord – buying somewhere – emergency accommodation – living at home – making your new place feel like home

As a general principle, universities like to put all new students in college-run accommodation, whether it's a hall of residence or a flat owned by a private landlord contracted to the university. However, thanks to the rapid expansion of higher education in recent years, this isn't always possible as the rise in student numbers hasn't been matched by an equivalent rise in accommodation. The situation is made worse in major cities by a shortage of accommodation in general, making what little there is extremely expensive.

The major cause of the problem is lack of funds. Some universities, though, are being quite enterprising and looking for alternative solutions – joining forces with housing associations to build new accommodation or leasing hard-to-let properties and flats in tower blocks from the local council. Other universities have resorted to drastic measures to house new students, putting them up in college sports and exam halls and even holiday camps.

This is hardly encouraging to new students, who find they have to add the potential spectre of homeless, for the first few weeks at least, to all the other initial uncertainties of college life. Not surprisingly an increasing number are adding another criterion to their list when choosing a college and course; the availability of accommodation. They are excluding cities like London and Oxford, where student accommodation has reached crisis point, and opting instead for universities where they have a better chance of having a place to live.

As student accommodation is often allocated on a first come first served basis, your chances of being offered accommodation are greater the earlier you send in your application. Do this as soon as your place on a course is confirmed. You may not have too long, especially if you got your place at the last moment through Clearing. Use your own initiative, too, to find accommodation. This chapter gives you plenty of ideas of how to go about your search.

APPLYING FOR ACCOMMODATION

Your college prospectus provides information about the range of college-run accommodation available (number of halls of residence, catering or self-catering, student houses, fees, facilities, distances from the main campus etc).

you're given a choice, go into
l. You meet so many people. It's a
od environment to go into straight
ay, and if you really don't like it,
 can always move out. You meet
 of people and it's a bit more
ure. You learn to cope on your
n, and to live with other people.
good training for when you have
hare a place in the second
r."

Rachel Eccles,
Town Planning student

When your course place is confirmed the college accommodation office will send you an application form to fill in and state your preferred type of accommodation and flatmates. You may also be required to provide a *guarantor*, who can be a parent, and who will guarantee to pay for any damage you cause during your occupation. Complete and return the form immediately. At some point in late summer you'll receive confirmation of your place, plus details of the fee and how to pay it.

If you don't hear from the accommodation office, telephone or write to them in case your name has gone astray from their list. Don't just assume that if you've got a course place you've automatically got a residential place.

Living in hall: pros and cons

If you're looking forward to leading a more independent lifestyle once you're away from home, the prospect of living in a hall of residence may seem restricting. However, halls aren't run like convents (they're often mixed for a start), and you're given a front door key so you can come and go as you please without being checked up on. Yes, there are rules, but they're to ensure everybody's safety, security and general well-being rather than restrict your freedom. Discipline is only ever likely to be applied if somebody abuses what is generally speaking a pretty easy-going and liberal system.

However keen you are to get set up in your own flat, if you're offered a place in hall take it like a shot. It'll give you a secure, ready-made home environment, a real bonus if you're living away from home in a strange city for the first time. Your room will be clean and warm and there will be useful on-premises amenities (most probably including a bar, laundry room, dining hall, TV and games rooms, plus bathroom and kitchen facilities on every floor). Your room will be fairly basic (a bed, desk and chair, easy chair, wardrobe, vanity sink and some bookshelves), but you are free, within reason, to stamp your own personality on it to make it feel like home. As halls usually employ cleaners, you get a regular hoovering and change of sheets.

> "Making friends was easy because I lived in hall. They laid on events especially, so people could get to know each other."
>
> Michael Poland,
> Applied Geology student

Living in hall works out cheaper than living in lodgings or a shared flat. Lighting, heating and water bills are included in the fee, and so is food – breakfast and an evening meal – if you're living in a catered hall. You pay each term's fee at the beginning, which takes care of the major part of your grant. But then, it's reassuring to know that whatever happens, you have a roof over your head and regular meals until the end of term. Also you only pay for your term-time occupation, not the holidays (unlike lodgings or a shared flat).

Another real advantage of living in hall is that you can start making friends from day one. There are students from a wide variety of backgrounds, studying all sorts of subjects, so you have a pool of potential friends far beyond the confines of your own department. It's a good way of spotting potential flatmates, too.

And the disadvantages? Well, halls can be noisy. Despite restrictions on playing music late at night, there's always one selfish prat who thinks they don't apply to him. And people will bang doors. Privacy can be difficult to come by, and there may always seem to be someone knocking at your door. There are times when you welcome the intrusion, but if you're trying to concentrate on an essay or revising for exams it can be a right pain. You can – possibly – solve this by sticking a Do Not Disturb notice on your door. One other disadvantage: the quality of meals in catered halls can vary quite considerably. So if your hall has a dining room, you may find the food bland, boring or very occasionally pretty foul – not to mention a waste of money if you miss meals regularly.

Living in a flat or lodgings

Not all universities have adequate hall facilities to house all new students (this is particularly true of the former polytechnics). So you may find yourself living in private rented accommodation instead in your first year. When your course place is confirmed the accommodation office should write and inform you what the options are (if they don't, contact them yourself). Many universities have their own pool of flats, houses and bedsits which they rent from the private sector and then allocate to students themselves. You'll receive a form asking you about your preferences (do you mind sharing a bedroom, sharing with smokers, sharing with students of the opposite sex etc). You'll then be allocated a place, and pay rent at the beginning of each term (usually to the accommodation office rather than the landlord). However, you'll be responsible for arranging for gas and electricity to be connected, and for paying the necessary deposits and bills (see Chapter 4).

"I came down a week before term started to look for a house, and found somewhere to share with four or five other people. Everybody clicked and got on really well, we were all on different courses. Within about a week we had quite a big social group."
David Collicut,
Town Planning student

FINDING YOUR OWN PLACE TO LIVE

If your college accommodation office can't place you directly, you will have to find somewhere yourself, with their help. Good accommodation tends to go quickly, so get organised and if at all

possible, spend some time flat-hunting before the start of term. The college accommodation office will have a list of recommended landlords and agencies, as will your student union. Check out also the noticeboards around college, small advertisements in local newspapers and advertisements in shop windows. An accommodation agency may require you to pay a fee once you've signed a tenancy agreement for a property on their books. Otherwise it's illegal for an agency to charge you a search fee.

Check on a map distances from college (you don't want to spend too much time or money travelling), make a list of possible places and telephone for an appointment to view. Dress neatly and be polite (landlords can pick and choose). You, on the other hand, may have to compromise. The kind of place you can afford to live on an inadequate student grant can come as a shock, especially if you've been used to a comfortable home environment.

Make sure you are safe

One thing you do not have to compromise on, however, is your safety. There has been rising concern in recent years about safety standards in privately rented accommodation, especially at the cheaper end of the market. It's undoubtedly true that some landlords couldn't give a toss about the safety of their tenants, for the main reason that it might mean having to spend some money. Nevertheless a landlord could be prosecuted for failing to comply with fire safety standards. He could be sued if his failure to maintain the gas, electricity and heating installations, or the general state of the property itself, resulted in the injury or death of a tenant (not that that's particularly consoling for the tenant).

Students are regarded as being particularly at risk precisely because they can only afford cheap (for which often read substandard) accommodation. Indeed, at the time of writing, two students were poisoned by fumes from a faulty water heater in their flat.

If you have any concern at all about the safety of your house or flat, you could try speaking first to the landlord or accommodation agency. If that doesn't succeed, contact your local fire station, who will be more than happy to come and inspect the premises and ensure the landlord does what's necessary to make the premises legally safe.

You should also ensure that your accommodation is reasonably secure against burglars and other intruders. Windows (especially on the ground floor) should fit securely and have appropriate locks. Your front door and the kitchen back door should have sturdy locks and bolts. If you have a room in a house which has other lodgers, you should have a lockable door.

The police are very keen to advise on matters of safety, especially as burglary victims often make life easier for the burglar through inadequate security. The Crime Prevention Officer at your local police station will be happy come round and check your general security – and maybe liaise on your behalf with your landlord for safety improvements, should it prove necessary.

> "I hated my first week because I was living in lodgings on my own. I think if I'd been living in hall it would have been different. I had trouble getting home at night because I was always going home on my own. It's very important for people who live in lodgings to make an effort to get to know people"
> *Nicola Buchan, History and Accounting student*

LODGINGS

Lodgings come in all types, good and bad. Some lodgings houses are run on a commercial basis, with rooms rented out to a number of individuals who may or may not be students. An increasing number of families and other householders are renting out a room to a student to make their own ends meet. Either way, the landlord lives on the premises, which has its own obvious restrictions.

It's important to check out several potential lodgings before committing yourself, because living at such close quarters can be awkward if you don't get on with the landlord or landlady. You could find it a bit lonely if you're the only student, and will have to make an effort to socialise with friends at college. The distance from college is also something to bear in mind, not only because of the time and expense in travelling, but the safety factor when you're coming home on your own late in the evening.

Lodgings will be more expensive than hall fees or the rent on a flat, as you will be paying for heating, lighting and baths. You will also be expected to pay a small retainer during the vacations.

Isolation and restrictions on freedom aside, you could have a really cushy time if you land up in good digs. Some landladies treat lodgers as part of the family, and this is something you can encourage to your advantage by being friendly and considerate in return (offering to pick things up from the shop if you're going yourself, move heavy pieces of furniture, that sort of thing). You may also get extra facilities free (eg laundry) by trading your own services (eg mowing the lawn, babysitting).

> "When you're looking for somewhere to share, the first thing to do is to find out who you can get along with. Ther are lists on college noticeboards, there's also a student housing list an there are agencies. The college accommodation office is quite helpfu but it's just overrun. There's such a massive housing problem in Oxford. They can't cope with the number of people looking for somewhere to live So you have to be prepared to look yourself"
>
> *Andy Camer*
> *Civil Engineering stud*

Things to check when you're looking for lodgings

☐ Does the price include breakfast only or is it full board (breakfast and an evening meal)? If it's not full board, can you have access to the kitchen to make your own meals? Are you restricted as to when you can do this (ie after the landlady has finished her own evening cooking)?

☐ Do you have to pay a retainer for vacations?

☐ Do you have your own front door key, and are there restrictions on how late you come home at night?

☐ Are you allowed a limited number of baths per week and can you take more if you pay for them? If you're sharing the family bathroom, can you only use it at certain times?

☐ Does your room have adequate studying facilities (ie a desk and chair, reading light and a place for your books)?

WHEN YOU FIND SOMEWHERE TO LIVE

You may feel pressured to make a quick decision to prevent the place being snapped up by someone else. However, don't sign anything without reading it through very carefully at your own pace (preferably without someone hovering over you), and having the legal aspects checked by your college or student union accommodation office. It's better to risk losing a potentially suitable place than to find yourself committed to a bad deal.

You may be required to pay a *deposit* (up to a month's rent) as a form of insurance against any damage you cause during your tenancy. This will be refundable when you finally leave, provided there has been no damage.

To protect yourself against unfair claims for damage (which does sometimes happen), you have a right to insist on an *inventory* of all the contents of your room/bedsit/flat.

Go through the list with the landlord or agent so that you're both agreed on the listed items. You should also inspect the room or property carefully for signs of wear and tear or damage. If a window pane is cracked, there's a cigarette burn on the carpet or a major scratch on a piece of furniture, have this added to the inventory before you sign it. That way you can't be penalised for damage you haven't caused.

If you have agreed to pay rent weekly your landlord or agent is obliged by law to provide you with a rent book. If you pay monthly or in full for a whole term, you must have a receipt as proof of payment. You can buy a rent book from a stationers to make your own entries (dated). Ask the landlord/agent to sign each time, especially if you're handing over cash. In the event of a dispute, it's important to be able to prove that you have paid all rent due, and on time.

Finally, if you are renting a flat or house you will have to arrange for gas and electricity to be connected for the day you move in, and for an account to be set up in your name (or joint names if you're sharing). You'll probably be asked to pay a deposit, which will be refunded when you vacate the premises. You'll have to bring all your own bedding and towels, as well as cooking utensils, plates and cutlery.

OBTAINING A TENANCY AGREEMENT

There are two basic types of tenancy agreement, an *assured tenancy*, which lasts indefinitely, and an *assured short-hold tenancy*, which lasts for a specific period (six months to several years). As a student you're more likely to be offered the latter, but either way, it's important to have something in writing (a) to protect you from being thrown out without proper notice and (b) to establish your and your landlord's obligations towards each other. Before you sign an agreement, get it checked, and anything you don't understand explained, by your college or student union accommodation office, or alternatively your local Citizen's Advice Bureau or legal centre.

There are certain grounds on which a landlord can ask you to vacate the property before the agreed tenancy period is up. He must give you at least two months notice if (1) he wants to occupy it himself or (2) if he defaults on his mortgage and the building society want repossession. He only has to give you two weeks notice if you're three months or more behind in paying rent or if you damage the property or its contents. If you don't comply with the landlord's notice to quit he can go to court to obtain a possession order. He is not legally allowed to evict you (or intimidate you into leaving) without first obtaining a court order.

"If there's a problem with the house it's up to the landlord to sort it out. You have to keep on at them. Our electrics blew up. Our agency had an emergency number you're supposed to ring. Nobody answered. I 'phoned up the normal number and left a message on the answerphone saying we'd called out the electricity board and we'd be sending them the bill, as we thought this was better than letting the house burn down. They sent someone round very quickly!"
Rachael Anderson, Tourism, Business and Management student

The landlord is also obliged to keep the property in good structural repair, both inside and out. If, for example, the plumbing fails, you should contact the landlord or agency and report the problem, and someone should be sent round to make the necessary repairs as soon as possible.

Although you will agree a rent with the landlord at the time of signing the tenancy agreement, you can challenge the rent afterwards if you think it's too high by contacting your local council's *rent officer*. If the rent is subsequently reduced, the landlord is bound to accept it. However, if you think your rent is fair, don't be tempted to ask for an assessment in the hope of getting it reduced even further. The rent officer has the power to increase it too, which you then have to accept.

PROBLEMS WITH YOUR LANDLORD

Do your best not to get embroiled in an acrimonious argument, especially if you feel your behaviour has been above board and your landlord is being unreasonable. Instead, seek advice from your college accommodation office, who can advise you on your legal rights and an appropriate course of action, and even deal with the landlord on your behalf. You'll fare better with the clout of the college authorities behind you.

Your existence can be made considerably more uncomfortable if you're living in lodgings, and having to face your landlord or landlady every day. Again, your best bet is to remain calm and reasonable and ask your college to intervene on your behalf. If you feel your relationship with your landlord has been irrevocably damaged, you may find it easier for your own peace of mind to look for alternative accommodation, rather than carry on living in an awkward atmosphere.

BUYING SOMEWHERE TO LIVE

As a student, you won't have the money, or the necessary record of financial stability, to obtain a mortgage, even if you were able to band together with friends to buy a property. However, if your parents have the spare funds and are willing to subsidise you, you could obtain a joint mortgage, with them acting as guarantors for the loan. Mortgage payments could be partially funded by taking in other students as lodgers. You and your parents would need to speak to a variety of high street lenders, banks as well as building societies, to find the best deal available. When you come to sell the property on graduation (assuming you move away from your university town), you may even have made a small profit.

EMERGENCY ACCOMMODATION: WHAT TO DO IF YOU HAVEN'T GOT A PLACE TO LIVE

University accommodation offices and student unions work very hard to find students places to live, but come the start of term there are inevitably some who begin college life homeless. Not only does this take all the fun and excitement out of one's new found independence, but it makes studying and getting to grips with a new subject a nightmare.

You're most likely to be at risk if you gain your place through Clearing (bearing in mind that you could obtain a place as late as the week before term starts). Not surprisingly some students can be forced to take drastic measures, either squatting in empty properties or, in one reported case, buying a second hand van to live in and parking it in a campus car park during term.

❒ Don't be afraid to keep on at your college accommodation office. It's the university's responsibility to find you somewhere to live, but the accommodation office may assume you've already found a place if it doesn't hear from you. As an emergency stop gap, you may be put up in a college gym. Take a sleeping bag and a few clothes, but don't take anything valuable as it could easily get nicked.

> "University-run houses tend to have a slightly higher standard of maintenance, and slightly cheaper rent. Some agencies charge fees. If you're in hall in your first year you're unlikely to get a university house in your second year. You have to find somewhere yourself. There are lots of private landlords, some of them very dodgy."
> *Rachael Anderson, Tourism Business and Management stude*

❒ If your family home is within reasonable commuting distance of college you'd be better off staying at home until you do find somewhere. The expense of travelling will be balanced to a degree by the saving in rent. The huge disadvantage is that it will seriously hamper your new social life and involvement in college activities at precisely the time you should be throwing yourself into party-going, discos and other freshers' events.

❒ If you have any relatives, family friends or even friends of friends living in your new town, ask if you can stay with them on a rent-paying basis for a few weeks.

❏ Is anybody from your school in the second or third year at your new college? They'll be renting a flat or house by now, and may be prepared to let you sleep on the sofa or floor for a couple of weeks on account of your former connections.

❏ Most university towns have YMCA and YWCA hostels where you can rent a room on a weekly basis. They offer excellent facilities and are consequently very popular, especially with overseas students.

❏ If your college is in a seaside town, or somewhere where tourism is a major contributor to the local economy, you may find landlords willing to rent accommodation (ie a holiday flat, caravan or room in a guest house) out of season. The major drawback is that you don't have the sort of legal protection an assured short-hold tenancy affords. But it is better than being homeless, and offers a short-term base for looking for more permanent accommodation.

LIVING AT HOME

If you're studying in your home town your LEA will expect you to live at home, whether or not this suits you or your parents, and will cut your grant accordingly. The LEA may make certain exceptions: if your parents are elderly or incapacitated; if you are already living independently away from home; if your family home is so far from college that you'd have to spend an unreasonable amount of time commuting.

You might be perfectly happy to live and study at home – there are, after all, lots of advantages. The environment is familiar, you'll already know a lot of people (although some of your school friends will have gone away to college), it'll probably be cheaper than living in hall or lodgings, you'll have free laundry facilities and, if you're very lucky, free, ready-cooked meals. You also won't have to go through the hassle of finding somewhere to live and the sort of time-consuming administration involved in living in a flat, such as remembering to pay bills, do the week's shopping and so on.

All this should help mitigate the disadvantages, of which there are several. You'll get a smaller grant (but it would all have gone on paying for accommodation and living expenses anyway). You may find that you live some way from the campus, so that you spend a great deal of time travelling and don't feel so much part of college life. But most important of all, you miss out on the experience and challenges of an independent life away from home, free from the parental gaze.

What about spending another three years with your parents?

Believe it or not, they may be as dismayed as you at the prospect of at least another three years together. The one thing that gets many parents through the inconvenience and awkwardness of their off-spring's teenage years is the prospect of said offspring leaving the proverbial nest to answer the distant call of further education. You may worry that living with your parents will cramp your style. You can be sure that their worry is that you'll be doing exactly the same to theirs.

What you all need to do sit down together and have a calm and reasoned discussion about any reservations you may have individually, and practical ways of solving them. Certain things may have to change. For example, you have every right to expect your status to be upgraded from being a 'child' to an adult; in particular you will expect more freedom in the way you lead your life, less parental supervision.

Similarly your parents – particularly your mother – may not be keen on having a 'child' around for a few more years at a time when they might reasonably have expected their practical responsibilities to have come to a natural end. On the other hand, they may be happy to have you living at home as an adult, which in turn will require certain adjustments in your behaviour (sharing in household tasks, for example, which you'd have to do if you lived independently). So long as you discuss things early on, before clashes or disagreements occur, you should have no trouble working things out.

Should you contribute towards your keep?

Don't assume you don't have to. Discuss it with your parents before you get your grant cheque. Obviously your room isn't going to be an additional cost for them, but there's your share of food, light and heating, telephone, washing machine, loopaper and so forth.

Just because the LEA has arbitrarily decreed that you live at home, it doesn't mean to say that your parents can necessarily afford to support you for what is quite a long period of time. Be sensitive to their financial situation (which they may not want to burden you with by bringing up), and make a reasonable offer. If they refuse it, all well and good. At least you've probably notched up some good will.

They may, however, gratefully accept. If you agree on a regular payment, keep to the schedule without being reminded (it's embarrassing and extremely irritating). You may find you have to find a part-time job to help make ends meet. But then, so do the vast majority of students.

POSSESSIONS AND MAKING YOURSELF AT HOME

Wherever you live, in a hall of residence or a shared flat, you'll want to add your own touches so it feels more homely. Before you transport all your worldly possessions to college, though, it's a good idea to (a) find out how much space you'll have to call your own and (b) what the security is like. The latter is especially important if you're going to be living in a shared flat because the kind of accommodation students can afford is usually in areas where burglary is rife. You should insure your possessions, wherever you live; the cost of replacing them far outweighs the expense of the insurance premium if you're ever unlucky enough to be burgled.

> "When you're sharing there's always going to be something that gets up your nose. I think it's quite interesting that people have diverse personalities, otherwise it would just get boring. There are the odd little niggles. Mostly it's a matter of people's personal habits."
>
> *Michael Poland, Applied Geology student*

Study-bedrooms in halls aren't as a rule spacious, so you're limited in what you can take with you. You'll have room for a radio, stereo system, TV, word processor or computer, a few personal books and clothes, and that's really about it. However there's usually a noticeboard you can pin things on, and you can put up posters (using Blu-tack, not Sellotape). To make your room even more cosy you could bring a colourful or ethnic bedspread and a cushion or two from home (you wouldn't be the first student to bring your teddy either!).

While a shared flat or lodgings may be spacier, the standard of furnishing and decoration can be pretty shabby, which you may find a bit depressing, particularly if you'll be spending quite a lot of your time there. It's worth spending a little effort and imagination in cheering the place up. You won't be able to decorate, so cover the walls with posters and see if you can borrow some cushions, bedspreads or even some old curtains to throw over chairs, sofas and beds. Even shabby places can look reasonably mysterious at night if you use side lamps and candles rather than bright overhead lights. Plants also contribute a homely dimension (although you have to remember to water them) and you may find you can buy them quite cheaply at a local market.

Wherever you live, be prepared for it to take a while to feel like home, especially if you've just come straight from a real, very comfortable one. It's surprising how just a few of your own bits and pieces can transform a place. Anyway, once you get into the swing of college life, studying and socialising, you'll be far too busy to sit around at home, moping about your surroundings.

Chapter 3

SURVIVING YOUR FIRST WEEK

Arriving at your hall or flat – finding your way around campus – who's who – getting to know your department – things you have to do in the first week – clubs, societies and the student union – making friends – getting on with your flatmates – advice for the mature student

Your first week at college, traditionally known as Freshers Week, is an event in its own right. Its sole purpose is to make you feel a part of college life from Day One, and you'll either love it or hate it! But however you feel, bear in mind that the first week is totally unrepresentative of what the rest of your time at college is going to be like. It's a time of feet-finding and making friends, and once that's out of the way, you'll be expected to knuckle down to work. Meanwhile, feel free to take the opportunity to establish your presence and, most important of all, have some fun.

Most students have a great time once they start getting over their initial nervousness. A few, however, find their first week or two a bit of a nightmare. It's partly because there's so much to take in on all levels, but mainly because students don't really know what to expect. Many colleges and student unions try to help by sending, in advance, useful information booklets and maps of the campus and the town. Some colleges put up signs around the place to help new students find their way around, and some even organise a rota of second years to give guided tours and answer questions. However, many colleges fall down badly in this respect, sending out inadequate information far too late, or, as often happens, simply doling out piles of information sheets on the first day itself. Pretty thoughtless really, since by this stage most new students are already suffering from information overload.

Knowing something of what to expect in the first few days at college gives your self-confidence a much-needed boost at a time when you're feeling confused and very obviously 'new'. That's where this chapter comes in. The aim is that nothing in your first week should come as too much of a surprise (with the exception of nice ones). It gives an idea of the numerous activities arranged especially in your honour to get you out and about meeting people. It outlines the tedious but necessary administrative chores you have to take care of (register, collect your grant and so on). It tells you how to find your way around college. And it also provides you with a run-down on the various academic and administrative staff you'll come across and whose job it is to help you get the best, academically, socially and personally, out of your next three years.

ARRIVING AT YOUR HALL OF RESIDENCE OR FLAT

If you're staying in a hall, you can usually arrive any time up to a couple of days before the official start of term. Someone will be on hand at the reception desk or administrative office to sign you in, tell you your room number and hand over keys. You can then spend time settling in and making yourself at home, exploring the hall's facilities and saying hello to the other arrivals.

If you're renting a flat you can usually move in any time up to a week before term starts. First you'll have to collect keys from the college accommodation office, agency or landlord. If you can, it's a good idea to spend a few days settling and getting to know your flatmates and local neighbourhood, getting in a supply of food and so on.

If you're living in lodgings find out if there are other students in the house before deciding when you want to arrive. If you're the only one, you may be happier moving in the day before term starts.

FINDING YOUR WAY AROUND CAMPUS

Expect to spend your first few days map in hand, trying to get from A to B without spending all day about it. Don't be afraid to ask for directions; more seasoned students and college personnel will be happy to help. With any luck, the places you'll need to find will be sign-posted, but here's a quick guide.

Your department

The centre of your universe (well, one of them) for the next three years. Here you'll find lecture room facilities, lecturers' offices, the department's administration office and a common room for the use of students.

The registry and the grants and loans office

You'll find these two places in the college's main administration block. In the first, you'll register once a year. In the second, you'll collect your grant cheque each term, apply for your Student Loan and also for hardship or access funds (see Chapter 5).

The library

Your major information source, and a peaceful and disciplined place to study. It may be open until quite late in the evening (depending on staff resources) and also over the weekend. If the library holds an induction course to explain how its various information retrieval systems function, do go on it (you'll waste valuable time trying to find out for yourself).

The student union bar, shop and offices

The focus of your social life on campus. The bar will have cheaper alcohol and snacks than you'd find in pubs (although the latter frequently have special promotion nights organised by their brewery when they're pushing a brand of beer). Most student unions also run a shop where you can buy stationery, second-hand books, tee-shirts, scarves, sweatshirts, sportskits and so on bearing the college logo and many other items. The union will also have its own administration offices from which it organises student-related events, and also where its counsellors can be contacted (the welfare

"I came from a town where there weren't many students. Oxford isn't as bad as other places, but there is a lot of student bashing. You go into town like you would at home, with a few friends, but there are student pubs and non-student pubs. The first few weeks we went into all different pubs and got into a few scrapes. You're immediately identifiable as a student. Everyone knows when the term starts and when students are going to be in town. It's very quiet in the holidays, and suddenly in come all the students into the pubs and immediately there's a conflict. It wasn't something I was aware of until I came here, but after a while you learn which are the student pubs and which aren't. It's a learning process."

Marc Holland,
Town Planning student

and accommodation officers, for example). The student union noticeboard is usually a rich source of information, exchanges and potential contacts, so check it out regularly.

The cafeteria

The college cafeterias and coffee bars are the places to go for a quick snack, a full meal or a coffee and a bun between lectures. The food is generally wholesome and filling rather than inspired. Prices vary from really cheap to just about high street caff level, depending on whether a college subsidises its cafeterias or expects them to run at a profit.

The careers office

An excellent source of information and advice on all the careers you can think of (plus some you probably hadn't). Your future career may not be uppermost in your mind in the first year, but if you aren't happy with your course and you want to transfer to another one within the college, the careers office will be able to help you.

The health centre

Most colleges have their own health centre on or near campus for the use of students and staff. You may find it more convenient to belong to your college health centre rather than your neighbourhood surgery because (a) you'll be in college most days and (b) you're more than likely to move to a different area in town in your second and third years. Health centre facilities tend to be comprehensive and will usually include services such as a general surgery, contraception, dentistry, psychiatric counselling, an optician and a dentist.

WHO'S WHO AT COLLEGE

A brief guide to some of the academic, administrative and support staff you'll come across during your time at college.

The vice chancellor
(also known as the dean, director, provost or principal)

The top dog, way beyond your social or academic sphere. He is the face of the college, responsible for ensuring the smooth running of the business side of things. The only occasion you're likely to come face to face with him is if you've brought the college into disrepute and you're about to be kicked out. There is also a chancellor, but he/she doesn't play an active role in college life, apart from handing out degrees at the award ceremony.

The registrar

He/she heads the team responsible for the smooth running of the student side of life at college, including admissions and grants.

The accommodation officer

A most important person, and one you'll have a lot of dealings with during your time at college. In the first instance the accommodation officer will help fix you up with a roof over your head for your first year, usually in college-run property (either a hall of residence or a flat). You'll also be able to get lists of suitable landlords and agencies when you have to find somewhere else to live in the second and third years. The accommodation officer will guide you through any legal document or contract when you do find somewhere, and advise you if you have a problem with your landlord.

The head of your department

Usually a professor (if fund allocations permit), and therefore a senior academic in his or her field. You may be invited for an initial chat some time in the first week, but you won't really have much to do with him or her on a day-to-day basis, unless he/she happens to give some of the lectures, or you have a major problem with your course.

The course tutor

The person in the department responsible for organising the content of your courses and co-ordinating the lectures etc. Also the person likely to haul you over the coals if you aren't pulling your weight academically.

Your personal tutor

One of the lecturers in the department will be assigned as your personal tutor, and you'll be invited for a private chat some time in the first few days. If you have any problems or worries at all, your personal tutor will be happy to lend a confidential and sympathetic ear and offer practical help and advice. It can be a problem with a relationship, health, accommodation, work, homesickness etc. Should you get into trouble with the law, or with other lecturers because your work is falling behind, he or she will intervene on your behalf. It's a good idea, therefore, to get some sort of relationship going with your personal tutor right from the start so that he/she will be even more motivated to help you if and when the time comes.

The warden

A hall of residence is administered by a warden, who usually lives on the premises for at least part of the time (there's usually a deputy warden, who's often a postgraduate student). You can speak to your warden in confidence about any problems you have with your accommodation (if, for example, your grant cheque is late and you can't pay your hall fees immediately), and also if you have any personal problems.

The college welfare officers and counsellors

All colleges have trained staff who specialise in helping students with particular problems, be they personal, health, legal, academic, financial or social. Advice is free and totally in confidence, and whatever you discuss, it won't be passed on to anyone else (eg your department) without your express permission. You can call by and make your own appointment (you may even be seen on the spot), or ask your personal tutor or warden to refer you.

Student union welfare officers and counsellors

Many student unions have their own trained counsellors, providing an alternative source of help and advice for any student with a problem. Student unions often run special confidential nightline telephone services, staffed by students, and offering sympathetic and confidential help.

> "You are generally given a week or so after Freshers Week to recover, and then the real work starts. I wish I had been more prepared for it. I found the change from A Levels fairly easy, but because of the size of the lectures it seemed more impersonal."
>
> *Mark Barnes,*
> *Humanities student*

GETTING TO KNOW YOUR DEPARTMENT

Your very first act on Day One is to go into your department and set about getting to know the people – lecturers and students – in whose company you'll be spending the next three years. There'll be no lectures as such, but you'll probably have an induction course or courses which introduce you to the ways of the department, the structure of the course and the course options. You'll also find out who your personal tutor is. Some departments organise a weekend away so that lecturers and students can really get to know each other on an informal and relaxed basis. This is an excellent idea, not least because the food is (usually) free and you have a chance to ask questions over a drink in the bar (which won't be free) and during meals, as well as during the informal lectures.

If you have any worries about your ability to cope with studying at degree level, now is the time to inquire if the college runs a study techniques course for new students. Your personal tutor should be able to point you in the right direction.

THINGS YOU HAVE TO DO IN THE FIRST COUPLE OF DAYS

If there's one overriding memory you'll have of your first few days at college, it will be queueing. Nothing so organised, either, as one super-queue, where you get all the necessary administrative bits and pieces done in one job lot. No, you will queue on several occasions, invariably in different parts of the campus. Look at it positively: it's an excellent way of (a) learning to find your way around college and (b) meeting the other people in the queue.

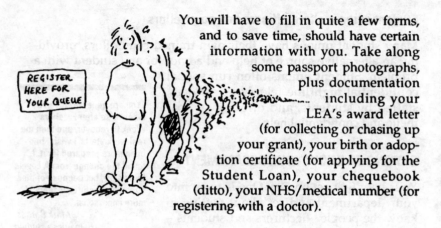

You will have to fill in quite a few forms, and to save time, should have certain information with you. Take along some passport photographs, plus documentation including your LEA's award letter (for collecting or chasing up your grant), your birth or adoption certificate (for applying for the Student Loan), your chequebook (ditto), your NHS/medical number (for registering with a doctor).

REGISTER HERE FOR YOUR QUEUE

Enrolling

This is the process by which you officially become a student. Where it takes place depends on the individual college, but it's usually at the registry. You'll receive proof of your newly acquired student status, which you'll need for when you register for other college facilities.

Collecting your grant cheque

In theory your grant cheque should be waiting for you. If it isn't, it's because your LEA hasn't sent it yet. Contact them immediately, quoting your award reference number to find out why not and when you can expect it.

Applying for the Student Loan

If your financial situation is such that you already know you're going to need extra money to make ends meet, you can apply for your Student Loan immediately. The procedure is quite complicated – see the relevant section in Chapter 5.

Registering with your student union

You automatically become a member of your college's student union when you register, and will receive a membership card. Keep it on you at all times, as you may be asked to prove your student status around campus for reasons of security. The card also entitles you to all sorts of discounts (you'll receive a booklet along with the card).

Register at the library

To be able to use the library's many facilities and take books out on loan you will have to register, bringing with you proof that you are officially enrolled as a student.

Register with the college health centre or a local GP

You will have to fill out a form with a few personal details, including the name and address of your GP back at home so that your medical records can be transferred. You will also have to provide your NHS medical number (this is different to your National Insurance number). If before your arrival at college, you've been sent, and have returned, such a form, your college may have already registered you with the health centre. Otherwise some time in the first couple of days you should go along to the health centre yourself, or alternatively a health centre/medical practice near to the campus.

Open a bank or building society account

That is, if you haven't got one already. You'll need a bank or building society account to pay your grant cheque into, and also for receiving your Student Loan (which isn't paid to you in person, but straight into your account by electronic transfer). See Chapter 4 for how to go about it.

CLUBS, SOCIETIES AND THE STUDENT UNION

The social life at university tends to be excellent, thanks to the extensive range of activities put on by the student union. Don't be surprised if in the first week in particular your feet barely touch the ground, as all manner of discos, parties and gigs galore are put on especially to get you in the swing of things. You won't have time to feel homesick!

One major event which you should make sure you attend is the Freshers (or Intro) Fair, at which the college's myriad clubs and societies vie for your membership. Joining a club is a good way of meeting people, and given the variety available at most colleges – sports, social, political, arts and special interest – you won't fail to find something that attracts you. Don't go mad and join everything in sight. Once you get down to work you won't have the time to be actively involved in more than a couple. More important, though, membership to an individual society can cost £10 or more, so you could waste a sizeable chunk of your precious grant on societies you end up never bothering to go to. If you're overwhelmed by the sheer choice, you don't have to make a decision there and then; you can join at any time during the term.

> "I'd just come off a Club 18-30 style holiday, so it was a bit of a shock. I missed Freshers Week being on holiday, so when I arrived everyone knew each other. I really feel I missed out by not going to Freshers Week. I think it would have helped a lot."
>
> *Rachael Anderson, Tourism, Business and Management student*

The student union

Much of your everyday social life – meeting friends, taking a break from your studies, finding out what's on when – will revolve around the student union; in particular, its bar and snack facilities. It's also the command centre for arranging social events, sporting fixtures with other colleges, the annual Rag Week and the production of the college newspaper.

The union is run by students on a grant from the college authorities. However, most unions have to supplement their grants with money-spinning and enterprising schemes in order to be able to fund administrative running costs, on-site facilities and the various student support schemes, both on campus and in the community, for which they're responsible.

College student unions vary in size, and in the range of social and sports activities and welfare services they provide. They're run democratically, with annual elections to appoint an executive committee comprising the union president, treasurer, secretary, welfare officer, entertainments officer etc. Some of these posts are sabbatical; the elected official takes a year off his or her studies and is paid (by the union) to work full time on behalf of members. Regular union general meetings, known as UGMs, are held throughout the term to debate social, political, environmental, topical and any other type of issue currently of concern (or in vogue) with members. As a member you can attend a UGM, contribute to the debate and vote on motions under debate. As with most things, the more people who attend UGMs, the more representative and democratic the decision-making process is. Be prepared to find that process a mixture of entertaining, sincere, boring and sometimes boorish, rowdy and occasionally very silly.

Most college student unions are affiliated to the National Union of Students, which provides training for student union officers and lobbies the Department of Education and Science and other government departments, political parties, local authorities and any corporate body interested in education.

MAKING FRIENDS

> "The first couple of weeks are the most important of your three years. You've got to get out and meet as many people as possible. If you don't, you can't pick and choose who your friends are going to be for the rest of the term."
>
> *Andy Price, Estate Management student*

Starting a new social circle from scratch is never easy, especially when you've got so much else to cope with. It's the one time you could do with being able to pop round to a friend's for a coffee and a chat and put your worries and new experiences into perspective.

It probably doesn't help much to say that everyone else is in the same boat, but it's true nevertheless. Some first years may look as though they've been there all their lives, but deep down inside everyone else will be feeling as apprehensive and shy as you. Freshers Week is designed to help break the ice by cramming so much activity into your first few days that you don't get a chance to sit in your room feeling lonely. Freshers Week provides you with the opportunity to get out and meet with people, but it's up to you to make the most of it.

It's important to make the effort to get out and socialise right from the start. If you leave it a few weeks, most people will have settled down into small social groups by then, making it much more difficult for you to break in.

If you're living in hall, make your first step knocking on the door of your neighbours either side and introducing yourself. That way you've got someone to go down to the hall dining room for your first meal. If your hall has a bar, invite your neighbour down for beer, or sum up your courage and go in by yourself. After your first lecture, ask the person sitting next to you if they fancy going for a coffee. When you eat in the hall dining room, or in the college canteen, don't head for an empty table but join a group of people where there's a spare place, and where you can get chatting. You'll find one of the easiest ways to start a conversation is to ask someone what they're studying and where they come from.

> "I was quite lucky because I had about five or six people I knew down here who were freshers as well. I was quite happy for the first couple of weeks, because I'd already got a set of friends. And then the group split up after about a month as they found different friends."
>
> Dave Smith,
> Chemistry student

Living in hall, you've got a rich and ready-made source of potential friends. It won't be quite so easy if you're sharing a flat, although you'll get to know your flatmates quickly enough, and will make friends through them as well. It will be most difficult of all if you're living in lodgings, especially if you're the lone student. Your main problems will be isolation and getting home at night after a disco or party, especially if you live some way from the campus. To begin with at least, your major source of potential friends may be your fellow course mates, but you should also make an effort to join clubs and societies.

When you first start talking to people be friendly and open, but resist the temptation to tell all and sundry the story of your life – not so much because you might bore them, but because many of the people you strike up conversation with in the first few weeks will turn out to be no more than passing acquaintances. It's wisest to keep your torrid secrets for the ones who actually become your real friends. A certain selectivity is always a good idea when making new friends, and this will be just about the only time in your life when you can pick and choose. Some people can be annoyingly difficult to discard when you realise you have nothing remotely in common but they don't seem to be able to take the hint.

> "In the first week everyone seems bright and cheerful and willing to make a good impression. It's been very easy to make friends here, because it's a very laid back environment."
>
> Emma, first year English student

Homesickness

However much you've looked forward to college, the newness and strangeness of it all can have you longing to take the first train back to family, friends and a familiar environment. Resist the temptation, especially the first weekend, because you'll miss out on a lot that's happening. This homesick feeling will pass, but while it lasts, throw yourself even more wholeheartedly into creating a busy social life. A bleak and basically furnished room can have a really depressing effect and increase your homesickness, which is why it's a good idea to bring a few of your own possessions along (colourful bedspread, posters etc) to make the place cosier and more comfortable.

If shyness is what's stopping you from making friends join a couple of societies or clubs. You'll feel more confident among people who share an interest, and as your main reason for going along is for the activity itself, the pressure to make friends is off. It won't be long, though, before you do.

If homesickness really is getting you down, don't keep it to yourself. College authorities are aware that life can be a bit too overwhelming for the new student, and that slotting into a swinging social life isn't the easiest thing in the world, even if you're normally a pretty outgoing sort of person. There are people you can talk to in confidence, and who will be sympathetic and understand how you're feeling. Your personal tutor is the most obvious person to have a chat with, but you can also talk to your hall warden (if you're in hall), or the college or student union welfare officer.

GETTING TO KNOW YOUR FLATMATES

The college accommodation office will, as far as possible, have teamed you up with reasonably like-minded people. That's not saying much, but if you put down on the form that you wanted to share with non-smokers the same sex as you, and you want a room to yourself, then that's what you should get.

Some colleges send you the names and telephone numbers of your flatmates before term begins, which is a good idea because then you won't be strangers when you meet. Even more usefully you can sort out practical things like having the gas and electricity supplies connected and who's going to bring what in the way of kitchen equipment etc.

Once college life gets properly under way you'll probably find your paths don't cross all that often, as everyone will have lectures and tutorials at all different times as well as their own personal social and leisure activities. However, it will help break the ice to spend some time together the day or two before college, either going out together for a drink or a cheap meal, or maybe getting in some beer, wine and pizza.

What you will also need to give some thought to is an informal agreement to make your living together bearable. It should cover such areas as bill-paying, shopping for essentials, setting up and paying regularly into a kitty for basic foods and items like toilet paper and washing up liquid, housework, having friends staying over night and so on.

> "I share a big house and get on pretty well with everyone. Though people keep nicking my food all the time, which really gets on my nerves, especially when I'm skint."
>
> Lee Knight,
> English Studies student

How to avoid getting on each other's nerves

What you may not be prepared for is living day-to-day with other people's personal habits, good, bad, irritating – and occasionally, if you're really unlucky, down right disgusting. Bear in mind that it works both ways. You may think you're a perfectly reasonable sort of person, but you never know what's likely to get up someone else's nose until they let you know in no uncertain terms. Typical bones of contention are:

❒ Leaving your washing up undone (especially if someone else has to do it before they can use the utensils)

❒ Not cleaning the bath after you

❒ Leaving the toilet in a less than pristine condition

- ☐ Not emptying ashtrays

- ☐ 'Borrowing' someone else's food

- ☐ Using the last of the milk, toilet paper etc without mentioning the fact, let alone actually replacing it

- ☐ Not paying your share of the bills on time

- ☐ Always borrowing money

- ☐ Running up huge bills on the telephone

- ☐ Being untidy in communal areas like the bathroom, kitchen or living room (what you do in your own room is your business)

- ☐ Not doing your share of the communal chores

- ☐ Having a boy/girlfriend staying regularly and who never contributes anything to the kitty

- ☐ Hogging the bathroom in the morning when other people have early lectures

- ☐ Playing music loudly late at night or when your flatmates are studying

- ☐ Making a lot of noise when you come home late at night when everyone else is in bed fast asleep (or was, until you turned up)

FITTING IN AS A MATURE STUDENT

If you are returning to your studies after a few years break, you may be feeling somewhat apprehensive about whether you'll have anything in common with all those fresh-faced 18-year-olds who, unlike you, have come straight from school and the parental bosom. What will come as a surprise is the comparatively wide range of ages of the people on your course, and at college in general. On some courses, and at some colleges, it's actually the 18-year-olds who seem the odd group out.

In fact, one in seven university students is classed as a mature student (the figure is even higher in the former polytechnics). The age definition of a 'mature' student differs from college to college, and from LEA to LEA, but generally speaking it's someone 21 or older, who has taken time out of education to work or bring up a family.

As a mature student, you have several distinct advantages over your younger colleagues. Statistically, you're likely to have chosen to study at a local college, which means you'll already have a home and a social life. Not for you the initial loneliness of wondering if you'll ever get to make friends. If, on the other hand, you are studying away from home you will have to start afresh like everyone else. But it won't be quite the ordeal it is for many younger students, thanks to your wider experience of socialising, working with colleagues and perhaps dealing with the general public.

Any worries you may have about your ability to get back into an academic lifestyle will largely be compensated for by your greater commitment and determination to study for a degree. You may already have completed an access course in order to qualify for your place at university, in which case you will have acquired recent experience of studying and researching and writing essays and reports. However, if you feel you need a quick crash course in studying techniques, many colleges provide study skills courses for first year students on which you can enrol.

"As what they call a mature student, I was a bit worried that I'd be a lot older than everybody else. I was expecting to see a load of pubescent teenagers running around trying to mate with everything – especially in the halls! There's a lot more older people starting college now."
Michael Poland, Applied Geology student (worked for four years before university)

If you do encounter problems, have a chat with your personal tutor. College authorities appreciate that mature students have special needs and problems and are usually willing to help if they can. For example, however disciplined you are in your personal studying, a sick child will understandably take priority in your life, at the expense of a lecture or an essay deadline. Any lecturer with a family of his – and particularly her – own is likely to appreciate that.

If you want to get the most out of your three or so years at university, by all means give your studies top priority, especially if the quality of your degree is important to you. But don't neglect the social side of your life. One of the great things about life on campus is that there's always so much going on in the way of subsidised entertainment, sports and campaigning activities. Obviously your ability to throw yourself whole-heartedly on to the social scene will be somewhat limited if you have a family. It may be a matter of being selective, rather than opting out altogether of the many opportunities open to you – eg foregoing the tiddlywinks club in favour of the debating society or the judo club. There's something else to bear in mind, too. You have a pool of classmates willing to supplement their grants by babysitting for you.

Chapter 4

YOUR GRANT: WHAT IT'S FOR AND HOW TO MANAGE IT

Taking full financial control of your life – working out a budget – basic bills and living costs – budget plan – insurance – opening a bank account – making friends with your bank manager – getting into debt – where to go for help – what to do if you are broke – cutting costs and saving money

Is that IT? So that was all that to your mother about the bare necessities ??

Collecting your first grant cheque is a bit like winning the football pools. All that money – hundreds of pounds – to spend on you and only you. And it's true – up to a point. But curb that impulse to rush out and buy a new music system or whatever else currently takes your fancy. There are a whole load of more mundane demands on your new-found riches. You'll be lucky if you can afford a new CD, come the end of term.

Let's be positive, though. When you graduate you'll have gained a qualification that will set you up for life. No, not your degree, but the ability to juggle your finances with a dexterity honed over three years of continuous ducking and diving.

YOU'RE IN CHARGE NOW

From your first day at college you will be expected to take full financial control of your life. Up until now, your fiscal obligations probably extended as far as buying clothes, magazines and music and generally having a good time with your friends. Being skint meant foregoing a night out at the pub until your next allowance or part-time wage packet was due. Bills, the week's food shopping, the rent or mortgage – all these boring but nevertheless essential aspects of everyday life were taken care of by your parents.

At college, however, you will be responsible for paying your own hall fees or rent, and then for food, travel, books, entertainment et cetera out of what remains of your grant. If you live in a rented flat you will also have to pay your share of gas, electricity and telephone bills. You may also be required to pay deposits for these services, as you most certainly will for your flat.

Once you've accounted for these necessities, there isn't a great deal left of your grant for the luxuries of life. Being skint as a student doesn't mean missing out a night at the pub. It means wondering if you can afford to eat next week.

WORKING OUT YOUR BUDGET

A grant is only intended to cover the most basic of living costs. It may do that – just about – if you learn how to manage it right from the very start.

First of all you'll need to work out a budget by making a list of all your basic *outgoings*, adding up the total and then deducting this amount from your *income* (your grant and any other money you may be receiving). What's left over will have to cover such expenses as books and stationery, travel, food and entertainment.

Work out your budget as soon as you're notified what grant you're getting. Then if your grant falls short of what you know your outgoings will be, you still have some time to find alternative ways of increasing your income (see Chapter 5).

> "My full grant just about covers the rent, and I'm left with £65 for the whole year."
> *Rachel Eccles,*
> *Town Planning student*

Base your budget on your grant only (but include any parental contribution or any other regular allowance you know you can count on). Don't, for the time being, include provision for an overdraft or Student Loan (unless you already know you're not receiving a full grant and will need to borrow). Keep these options in reserve for an emergency.

WORKING OUT YOUR BASIC LIVING COSTS

Although you won't receive your grant until you're actually at college, your LEA will have notified you beforehand how much you'll be getting, including how much (if anything) your parents are expected to contribute.

When you receive confirmation of accommodation, you'll also be informed what your rent will be for the term. You'll be required to pay this in a lump sum at the beginning of each term, which you'll find immediately takes care of the major portion of your grant. If you have to find your own place to live, your college or student union accommodation offices will be able to give you an idea of the cost of local flats and lodgings.

"The first year wasn't so bad financially because I was in a hall and it's much cheaper. In fact it makes a considerable difference. You're not paying for holidays, bills or heating. Launderette facilities are much cheaper."

*Rachael Anderson,
Tourism, Business and
Management student*

If you're living in a hall of residence you only pay for your term-time occupancy. If you're renting private accommodation, however, you'll be expected to pay rent for the full year, including vacations. Obviously this puts an additional strain on your financial resources. You might consider looking for vacation work in your university town rather than at home, so that at least you're not paying for an empty flat for large periods of the year.

If you're renting from a landlord you may have to pay a deposit or *key money* for the flat. You'll get this refunded when you finally vacate the flat – provided you haven't done any damage.

Gas, electricity, water and telephone bills

If you have a place in a college hall of residence, your light, heating and water bills will be included in each term's rent. Public payphones will be available.

If you are renting a flat or house from a private landlord you will be responsible for arranging gas and electricity supplies to be connected, which will invariably involve paying

"For our telephone we have a chart a we write down all our own calls, whether it's local or national, peak tin standard or cheap. We also get an itemised bill, which helps."

*Rachael Anders
Tourism, Business
Management stuo*

a (refundable) deposit. You will then pay the bills on a quarterly basis. The water supply will already be connected, but you will receive water rates twice a year (although sometimes this is included in the rent).

If you want a telephone you'll have to arrange and also pay for it to be installed/ connected. Be warned that telephones are notorious for running up huge bills, especially in a communal flat, and consequently can become a cause of friction. You can remove the temptation by installing (a) a payphone or (b) a telephone that only takes incoming calls.

When you finally vacate a flat remember to collect all the refunds due to you, and especially important, to have all supplies disconnected on your last day (otherwise the new tenants may run up bills on your accounts).

What if you can't pay a bill?

Don't put it in a drawer and forget about it. And don't leave it until the last minute to admit your plight, but contact the customer enquiries number on your bill and explain your situation. Explain exactly (ie honestly) what the problem is (maybe your Student Loan cheque or parental contribution has been delayed), and when you'll be able to pay. Provided you take the initiative to contact them early, the gas, electricity, water and telephone companies are generally willing to be helpful, either by extending your payment deadline or switching you to their particular 'budget', or instalment, form of payment. A lot of people have problems paying their bills these days, so there's no need to be embarrassed. You'll find it much more embarrassing – not to mention expensive and inconvenient – to be cut off.

> "There can be lots of problems with bills, especially whose name a bill is in. I've known houses where they don't pay the bill and then everyone moves out at the end of the year, leaving the one person, whose name the bill's in, with a wacking great bill."
> *David Collicutt,*
> *Town Planning student*

Television/video/TV licence

Halls of residence invariably have TV lounges, but privately rented flats or houses may or may not have a TV for your use. If you want a set for your room in hall, or your flat doesn't possess one, it's easy to rent one.

Radio Rentals, which has shops all over the country, has a special deal for students which allows you to rent a set (and a video too) for nine months, in other words the length of the academic year – and for half the rental rate during the summer holidays. Renting has a particular advantage in that if something goes wrong with the set repairs are made (or it's replaced) free of charge. Otherwise repair bills can be very high. You can also hire kitchen equipment, such as washing machines and tumble dryers, from them.

> "For our telephone we have a chart and we write down all our own calls, whether it's local or national, peak time, standard or cheap. We also get an itemised bill, which helps."
>
> Rachael Anderson,
> Tourism, Business and
> Management student

Your parents' TV licence doesn't cover a set you take with you to college (nor does your hall of residence's if it has a TV lounge). You will have to buy your own (currently £83 per annum for a colour licence).

Council Tax

Full time students (including student nurses) are exempt from paying the council tax.

Budgeting when you're sharing a flat

Everybody shares responsibility for ensuring the utilities are paid on time (you'll be cut off if you don't, and charged extra for reconnection). It makes sense to elect one person to take charge of such matters, perhaps rotating each term so it doesn't become too much of a burden.

So that the designated bill-payer doesn't have to constantly hassle you all for money when bills become due, consider each putting aside some money at the beginning of term, preferably in an interest-bearing bank or building society account that's held in all your names (any cheque should be signed by at least two of you).

Food

If you're living in a catered hall of residence the hall fee will probably include breakfast and an evening meal. You'll have to budget for all other meals out of your grant.

If you're sharing a flat you'll have to organise all your own meals. Unless you and your flatmates lead wildly varying lives and as a result rarely cross each other's paths, it makes sense – and saves quite a bit of money – if you plan to eat some meals together and co-ordinate your food shopping. You'll need to agree on a certain sum of money which everyone will pay into a kitty each week, and also be quite specific about the type of things it's meant to be used to buy – basics like potatoes, coffee, bread and so on. If you have a predilection for smoked salmon, you'll have to pay for it yourself!

> "Nicking food is a problem in quite a lot of places. I know a house where there's a couple of people that have financial problems. They won't pay gas and electricity or telephone bills on time. They won't have enough food in either, so they'll start 'borrowing' off other people. That causes a lot of trouble and friction."
>
> Andy Price,
> Estate Management student

If you don't have a great deal of experience in catering for yourself see Chapter 6 for general advice on shopping, pricing and cooking.

Remember to make an allowance for holidays

Your grant is intended to cover vacations, and as a student you aren't entitled to receive social security benefit. You may find it more practical to try and find a job to support yourself through the holidays and concentrate your grant on term time expenditure.

INSURANCE

You may think you don't have anything worth insuring, but imagine for the moment that you get back to your room and find all your possessions gone. Now think about what it would cost to replace them. There's your stereo, music collection, books, television and video recorder, computer or word processor, guitar – so you could be talking about having to replace around £2,000 worth of possessions.

BUDGET PLAN

1. *Your income each term*

        £

Grant   _____

Parental contribution   _____

Any earnings/savings   _____

Other (ie allowance from grandparents)   _____

Total for the term   _____

To find your weekly income divide the term total by the number of weeks in the term:

2. *Your outgoings (per week)*

        £

Rent/hall fees   _____

Food and drinks   _____

Any deposits (flat, gas, electricity, telephone) _____

Gas bill   _____

Electricity bill   _____

Telephone bill   _____

Transport   _____

Books, materials, equipment and stationery _____

Insurance   _____

Car/motorcycle running costs   _____

Entertainment   _____

TV licence   _____

Other   _____

WEEKLY TOTAL OUTGOINGS:

If your weekly outgoings exceed your weekly income, go through your expenditure again and see where you can trim it further. If your outgoings still aren't covered, you will have to find a way of increasing your income. For suggestions on how to do this, read Chapter 5.

Unfortunately students make easy targets for burglars because they are known not to be very security-conscious, and they tend to live in insecure digs in high risk areas. Insurance companies know this from experience, and accordingly charge fairly high annual premiums for student policyholders – currently up to £100 per £1,000 pound of cover if you're in private rented accommodation. The cost should be rather less if you're living in a hall of residence, where security is generally tighter.

Insurance may seem like money down the drain – until you have to make a claim, that is. It's worth checking your parents' contents insurance policy to see if your possessions will be covered while you are away at college. If they're not, it may be possible to extend the policy's cover for an additional premium so that it does include your possessions. Otherwise your student union will have a list of insurance companies prepared to cover students.

Read the policy's conditions and small print carefully. Specific types of claims may be excluded; for example, if you are burgled your claim may only be paid out if there are signs of a break-in, not if you've left a widow open or forgotten to lock your door. Some policies don't allow you to claim for lost contact lenses or sports equipment, or thefts from vehicles. If you have anything of particular value, you may be required to list it separately, possibly even pay an additional premium. Bicycles, being eminently nickable, almost always require separate cover.

Travel insurance

If you're travelling abroad in the vacations, or studying overseas for a short period, you must buy travel insurance to cover not only things like lost luggage but doctor's, medical and hospital bills, all of which can be extremely expensive. Make sure that, in the event of serious injury or illness, the policy includes provision for an air ambulance home. The cost of a policy is cheap at the price, at around £25 for a month's cover.

Life assurance

This is a form of insurance which pays a lump sum to designated dependants on the death of the policyholder. Resist any attempts by an insurance company to sell you one. Unless you are a mature student, it's unlikely at this stage in your life that you have any dependants (ie children, a spouse or partner), so it would be a waste of money.

OPENING AN ACCOUNT WITH A BANK OR BUILDING SOCIETY

If you haven't already got a bank or building society account, open one before you arrive at college. You'll need it to pay your grant into, and also for the purpose of acquiring a Student Loan. It will help you in your budgeting.

Realistically, you'll need an account which has the option of an overdraft facility. An ordinary building society savings account is unlikely to be flexible enough for your practical requirements, plus cheques take around ten working days to clear, which can seem a lifetime when you need to get at your money. The choice, therefore, is between a straightforward bank account and a building society current account.

When you open an account you'll be given a chequebook and, depending on the bank, a cashcard to guarantee cheques up to a specified limit (some banks require you to apply for a card). You'll be sent regular statements to help you keep tabs on your money. You are also given a *personal identity number* (PIN) number, which enables you to withdraw cash outside normal banking hours from cash machines, check your balance and order a statement or a new chequebook.

The advantages of a special student account

Believe it or not, banks are competing vigorously for student customers. You are the high earner of the future, and therefore a prime target for their other, immensely lucrative (for them) financial products. Accordingly they offer special *student accounts*, combined with incentives designed to attract your attention. They are publicised in the summer, and vary in what they offer, so it pays to shop around. Even if you already have an account, do consider switching it to a student account, either at your current bank or elsewhere if the terms are better.

A student account offers useful financial concessions not available to other customers, which at the time of writing include: interest on the money in your account; no charges on standard transactions or on arranging overdraft facilities; interest-free borrowing up to a certain level and preferential rates (eg cheaper than the standard rates) thereafter and so on. If you do have to arrange an overdraft or loan, a student account will save you a small fortune on interest charges and fees (a bank charges around £75 for 'arranging' a non-student overdraft facility!).

> "I don't get a full grant, but what I got lasted about two weeks. Rent, food, books and socialising puts a big hole in your grant."
>
> *Lee Knight,*
> *English Studies student*

Each bank also offers a 'free gift' to tempt you to open an account. It's up to you to compare the relative value of the gifts on offer, but you might, for example, ask yourself if a free rail-card or a cash sum might be of more practical use than a record token or free driving lesson, or whatever else the special offer might be at the time.

There are a couple of other advantages in having a student account. From the convenience point of view, many banks have branches on or near campus, and these often have a specially allocated staff member who's familiar with the problems of student life. Theoretically at least, you're more likely to receive a sympathetic ear at a campus branch, than at an 'ordinary' branch, where an impoverished student will be regarded as the lowest of the low.

Keeping track of your expenditure

If you are to keep to your budget you must know where your money goes – and exactly how much you have in your account at any time. You might find it useful, especially in the beginning, to make a note of your daily expenditure.

Always fill in your cheque stubs and keep up a running total. It can pay – literally – to go through your bank statements, as banks often make mistakes. If you get cash from a cashpoint remember to make a note in your chequebook and deduct it from your running total.

Most bank cards have a *Switch* or *debit* facility, which means you can pay for goods at a shop or supermarket without writing out a cheque, the amount being electronically deducted from your account. As with cashpoint transactions, it's easy to forget you've spent the money, and you can get a shock when it appears on a statement, so make a note of the transaction.

Beware credit cards

These are responsible for more debt and misery than can be imagined. Apart from the fact that they have an uncanny knack of encouraging even the most thrifty people to spend with abandon, they are the most expensive may of borrowing money (which is what credit is), other than having an unauthorised overdraft or going to a loan shark. The high street banks have also abolished the interest-free credit period if you don't pay off your balance in full each month, which means that interest is charged on an item from the day you bought it. With a sizeable sum of interest being added every month, a credit card debt is depressingly difficult to pay off.

Keeping your money secure

Each year many millions of pounds are lost through stolen chequebooks and cash and credit cards. All too often the legitimate account holder is the loser. True, cheques can be stopped if you discover the loss in time, but trying to recover money lost through a so-called 'phantom withdrawal' at a cashpoint is another matter. As far as all banks are concerned, it's up to you to prove you haven't made your card available to someone else, and that's almost impossible.

So take a few simple precautions.

☐ Never carry your chequebook and chequecard together in the same pocket or wallet.

☐ Memorise your PIN number. Never carry a record of it on your person or in a diary – and *never* let anybody else have it.

☐ If you're withdrawing money from a cashpoint, don't key in your PIN number in full view of others. Don't count the money in public. If you're withdrawing money after dark remember that you are very vulnerable.

☐ If you lose your chequebook or cashcard or have either of them stolen you must get them cancelled as soon as possible.

Contact your bank, or if it's out of office hours, call their 24 hour lost/stolen telephone number.

MAKING FRIENDS WITH YOUR BANK MANAGER

While you've been living at home your contact with your bank is likely to have been restricted to transactions with the cashpoint outside. You may never have had any need to meet your manager.

Be prepared for this to change once you're at university. Juggling your finances on a small income is never easy, particularly if you're new to it, and if you find you're having difficulties making ends meet you may need some expert advice. If it's simply a matter of working out a budget to keep your expenditure under control and looking for ways to econo-mise, your college or union welfare officer will be happy to help. But if you need a small loan to tide you over, you'll need to make an appointment to see your bank manager, or more likely the student account manager.

If the prospect fills you with apprehension, it's probably because you share the common view that a bank manager is a humourless, unpitying excuse for a human being who will take great delight in watching you grovel. In their defence, banks would argue that they are often forced to turn the metaphorical screws because customers don't have the courtesy to ask for permission first before going into the red.

It will make your life a great deal easier if you can get your bank manager or student manager on your side before you need to ask them a favour. You can do this by (a) dropping by and introducing yourself at the beginning of your first term, on the principle that they'll be more sympathetic if you're not a stranger to them, (b) keeping them informed of your financial situation, especially if you think you might be heading for trouble, and (c) operating your account in a responsible manner and not overdrawing without asking the bank first.

Campus branches in particular know from experience that life is tough for a student, money-wise. Treat your bank decently and there's no reason why your dealings with it should ever be an ordeal.

GETTING INTO DEBT

Living on a grant for the next three years isn't going to be easy, but in a perverse sort of way, that's part of what being a student is all about. There are hours of fun to be had, bemoaning your impoverished lot with your peers in the college canteen. It's one of the things that binds you together – and it's the only time in your life when being poor is something of a social cachet.

> "I've just had my bank overdraft cancelled because I haven't paid anything into my account for four months. I'm only paying it off £20 a month, but it means I'm living off my credit card at the moment. And that's costing me £30-40 in interest a month. I haven't got a choice, it's that or nothing. I was in a lot of debt at the end of the first year, and I've been using my grant cheques to pay off my debts at the beginning of term, so I've never had the money to go into the bank at the beginning of term."
>
> *Andy Cameron,*
> *Civil Engineering student*

Looking at things realistically (always the best course when dealing with finances), your chances of avoiding getting into debt at some point during your college career aren't great, even if you manage to operate on the strictest of budgets. For many students the critical year is the final one, when vacation or term-time jobs are, understandably, suspended in favour of all-out studying for finals. A third of students are in debt at any one time, and according to one of the major banks most will graduate owing on average £1,100.

You may be able to avoid debt – and you can certainly minimise it – by having built up some savings before you arrive at college, working out and sticking to a weekly budget, and finding a part-time job during term-time and working during vacations.

Who can you turn to for help and advice?

If you have never had to organise your finances before, or you're having difficulty making ends meet, don't be afraid to ask for help. There are people who understand the sort of problems and pressures that you're facing and can offer practical help and advice.

If you're not sure who to speak to have a word first with your personal tutor, who'll point you in the right direction. However, your college or student union welfare officer is experienced in dealing with financial problems. You can also speak to your bank manager, or your branch's student account manager, who will be sympathetic and helpful (provided you've been running your account responsibly).

Whoever you speak to, you'll be treated in confidence and with respect. But do try to ask for advice or help *before* you get into difficulties. You'll save yourself sleepless nights and unnecessary angst, and a problem is invariably easier to sort out the earlier it's confronted and tackled.

WHAT TO DO IF YOU ARE BROKE

Don't stick your head in the sand, hoping your problems will go away. They won't. They'll get worse. Seek help and advice as soon as possible.

- ❐ Go see the college welfare officer. Every college has special *Access* or *Hardship* funds (more of which in the next chapter), and he or she may be able to help you obtain some money from these.

- ❐ Go and see your bank manager, who may be able to help you through your immediate difficulties with a small overdraft facility.

- ❐ If you haven't already drawn up a budget, do so now. This will show you exactly where your money has been going (it's the easiest thing to fritter away), and where you can start making economies.

- ❐ Don't try economising on food (unless you've been buying expensive takeaways or pre-cooked meals). Try and cut down on cigarettes and alcohol instead.

- ❐ Read carefully the following section on cutting costs and saving money.

Cutting your everyday living costs

Living on a strictly limited budget requires discipline and imagination right from the start. The next chapter has ideas on increasing your income, but there are also lots of ways you can minimise your everyday expenditure.

❐ If you take out money from your account as and when you need it you'll find it much harder to keep track of what you spend. You'll find the money always seems to get spent somehow, too! Work out how much you need to cover your everyday living expenses

> "I spend between £30-£50 a week on cigarettes and alcohol, which is pretty much the same for a lot of people. Most people I know have gone past their overdraft stage by the second term and are into their student loans."
>
> *Debbie Batt,*
> *Business and Finance student*

for one week. Withdraw that amount from your account *once a week*. Save yourself from further temptation by allotting yourself a daily allowance and only carrying that on you.

❐ Do try to stick to your budget. If, though, you find you really have to borrow to make ends meet, take advantage of your bank's interest-free concession on student accounts. Never go into the red without permission as the interest rate on unauthorised borrowing is punitive – only adding further to your financial burden.

❐ Do insure your worldly possessions. Not to do so is a false economy – which you'll find out if you're ever unfortunate enough to have anything nicked. Shop around for the best priced policy without compromising on your cover (ie the cheapest may not be the best).

❐ Save on fares to college and buy yourself a second hand bike.

❐ There are some circumstances under which you can claim your travelling expenses: (a) if you are disabled (b) if your course requires you to spend a period overseas and (c) if you are studying medicine or dentistry and you have to attend an establishment away from your main place of study.

❐ If you are a mature student, you may be eligible for an additional grant. Check with your LEA.

❏ Buy a Young Persons Railcard and a Discount Coach Card and save a third of all your fares.

❏ Check out the discounts your NUS membership entitles you to. There are sure to be some at local shops and stores. Buy an International Student Identity Card, which entitles you to discounts on travel, food etc in the UK, and elsewhere.

❏ If you are sent a booklist by your department before you arrive at college hold off buying anything until you find out exactly what's vital to your course. Text books are expensive, even in paperback, and you could easily spend a major portion of your grant on books which turn out less than vital to your course – while queueing at the library along with thirty or so of your coursemates for a single copy of a crucial book it would have paid you to buy – if you'd had any money left. You may be able to buy some books second hand when you get to college. Check out the department notice board, college/student union book sales and second years who may be interested in selling you their own copies.

> "Books are very costly. Especially as at the start of the first year they giv you a reading list of about a 100 books, and people go out and buy half of them – only to realise they didn't need any of them. I only bought five books in my first year, which cost me over £100, and I've only got about three creases in the spines."
> *Andy Price,*
> *Estate Management student*

❏ Save money on stationery (paper, folders etc) by taking advantage of high street stationers' 'Back to School' promotions in late summer/early autumn. Your student union shop may also sell stationery at discount prices.

❏ Don't go mad in Freshers Week and join every club and society in sight. You'll probably only have time for a couple at the most once you get into your studies – and at £10 or more a club to join that's an awful lot of money down the drain.

❏ Buy clothes from charity shops. Generally speaking, the best quality stuff is to be found in the posher neighbourhoods, and the best items get snapped up quickly, so look in regularly.

☐ Make full use of your college and student union cafeterias and bars. In most colleges the food and drinks are subsidised and cheaper than off campus.

☐ Keep an eye out for beer promotions in local pubs. When brewers introduce a new beer they often have a half price period to get the punters interested.

☐ If you are a regular beer drinker, why not brew your own? All-in kits are inexpensive (as is the very basic equipment required) and easy to use. Depending on the price of the kit, you could be drinking your own beer for less than 20p a pint!

☐ Make the most of on-campus gigs, discos and other entertainments – they're cheaper and often more fun because you know more people.

☐ Cinemas and theatres often have price concessions. If in doubt, ask.

☐ If you are in self-catering accommodation, learn to cook. It's cheaper than eating in cafés and pubs, and *much* cheaper than buying TV dinners and pre-cooked meals from the supermarket.

> "I share a student house with three other people. We do our food shopping once a week, and always go in pairs so that if one person is tempted to add things to the trolley that aren't on the list, the other one can stop him or her. So far it's worked quite well."
> *Ross Anderson, English Studies student*

☐ When shopping for food use open air markets wherever possible and supermarkets rather than expensive (if convenient) corner shops. Learn to compare prices between brands etc, and keep an eye out for special offers and price reductions (especially towards the end of the day and at the weekend). Avoid buying things on impulse. Make a list beforehand and stick to it. If you're sharing a flat, shop in pairs it helps keep you on the straight and narrow. See Chapter 6 for more ideas on shopping and eating cheaply.

Chapter 5

MAXIMISING YOUR INCOME

*Applying for a grant – your parents' contribution – additional LEA
allowances – earning and saving – obtaining an overdraft – the Student
Loan – borrowing from your family – access and hardship funds –
sponsorship – working during term and vacation – getting help from the
state – taking a year off to earn money*

Living away from home is an expensive business – however carefully you budget. You need to start planning your finances and exploring all potential sources of income long before you arrive at college. The first step is to find out if you are eligible for a grant from your LEA, and you should apply as early as possible in the year you want to go to college. Your school will give you an application form, plus a copy of the Department of Education's free guide, *Student Grants and Loans*, which gives the latest grant rates, as well as a lot of other useful information.

Don't wait until you've been offered a place on a course before applying (which could be as late as September if you go through Clearing). Grant applications can take weeks to process – local authorities are increasingly hard-pressed and many don't regard students as uppermost on their list of priorities.

It's government policy to make students and their families share some of the responsibility for financing their education. So even if you are one of the lucky but dwindling band of students (currently about one in four) who receives a full grant, the first thing you have to realise is that it won't be enough to live on. You are expected to supplement it with a Student Loan (which you repay after you graduate), your own savings and part-time and vacation earnings, and anything your parents contribute (over and above the LEA-decreed *parental contribution*). If this still isn't enough, there are other sources of financial help – more of which later.

APPLYING FOR A MAINTENANCE GRANT

Regardless of your family's financial status, your tuition costs will be paid by your LEA, direct to your college. Your maintenance grant, which is intended to cover all your living costs while at college (and during the holidays), is paid direct to you. However it is *means-tested*, which means that the LEA takes into account your parents' income (or if you are married, your spouse's) before deciding whether you are eligible for a grant, and if so, how much.

The rate for the 1993/94 academic year is £2,845 for students living away from home and studying in London, £2,265 if they're studying outside London, and £1,795 if they're living at home.

To be eligible for a grant you must have lived in the UK for the three years before the academic year in which your course begins (unless you or your family were working temporarily abroad during this period). You must not have received a grant before, either. There are exceptions though, so do ask your LEA for advice. For example, if you changed a course or college within a specified time you could still be eligible for a full grant for your new course (see the chapter on changing courses for more details).

The parental contribution

Your parents will be required to fill out a financial statement detailing all income for the previous financial year. If their earnings have fallen in the meantime, it's important they make this absolutely clear to the LEA, or they'll be assessed on an unrealistically high figure. Your parents can refuse to fill out a financial statement, but if they do, your LEA won't give you a grant.

Allowances are made for specific outgoings such as mortgage interest payments, the cost of supporting other children, pension schemes and so on. What's left when these are deducted is known as your parents' *residual income*, and this is the figure the LEA uses to work out your grant entitlement, and how much, if anything, your parents are expected to contribute. According to the 1993/94 rates your parents will start coughing up money if their residual income is as little as £13,630 (they'll contribute £45 a year). The contribution increases on a sliding scale until it reaches the full amount of the student grant – by which point you you don't get any grant at all and your parents are expected to support you fully.

But what if your parents won't pay?

The National Union of Students has estimated that around a third of students expecting a contribution from their parents receive nothing at all. Of the rest, one in ten receives less than they should.

One of the major problems is that what a LEA decides a student's parents should contribute to make up a grant and what they can actually afford may be two entirely different things. This is especially true in a recession, when a parent's income may have decreased substantially or even ceased altogether as a result of redundancy. There have been instances where an LEA has refused to reassess the grant awarded in the light of a family's changed financial circumstances.

Not all LEAs are so hard-hearted though, so if your parents suffer financial hardship at any time in the academic year, it's certainly worth asking your LEA to reconsider your grant.

But what if your parents are merely being tight-fisted?

If your parents can afford to contribute to your grant but are refusing, this puts you in a tricky position, as there's no way they can be forced to honour their obligation. There are parents who think their financial responsibilities to their offspring end the day they finish school.

By all means try moral blackmail. If that fails (someone who's hard enough to deny financial support to the fruit of their loins in the first place isn't going to be easily swayed), you really have no choice but to look for other ways to increase your income.

Applying for a grant as an independent student

There are circumstances in which your LEA will regard you as an independent person, and as such your parents won't be required to contribute to your upkeep.

- ❏ If you are 25 or over before the course starts.
- ❏ If you have been married for at least two years before the course starts (though your partner's residual income will be assessed and he/she may be required to make a contribution to your grant).

☐ If you have supported yourself for three years before the start of the course.

☐ If you have lost contact with your parents.

☐ If you are in the care of a local authority or voluntary organisation.

YOU MAY QUALIFY FOR EXTRA FINANCIAL HELP FROM YOUR LEA

There are circumstances in which your LEA may be prepared to give you some extra money if you're receiving a maintenance grant from them (the allowances are means-tested). Contact them as soon as you think you may be eligible – not all LEAs will award additional allowances retrospectively.

☐ **If your course is longer than the standard academic year** (25 weeks and 3 days at Oxford and Cambridge, 30 weeks and 3 days at most other colleges) you can apply for an allowance to cover the extra time you spend studying. It's up to you to inform your LEA, who will send you a form that requires your college to confirm the dates.

☐ **If your course requires you to study abroad for at least a term** you can apply for help with your travel costs, plus an additional maintenance allowance to cover the greater living costs you're likely to incur living in a foreign country. Your LEA can give you more information (the amount varies according to the country), plus a form for your college to confirm the details.

You may also be eligible for a European-funded grant, such as ERASMUS, LINGUA or COMETT. See the chapter on studying abroad for more details.

☐ **If you are a mature student** (26 and over) and you have earned at least £12,000 (or you've received this amount in taxable state benefits) during the three years before your course starts, you may qualify for an extra allowance on top of your grant. The allowance is on a sliding scale according to your age, starting at £280 aged 26, and going up to £980 aged 29 and over 1993/94 rates).

☐ **If you are a disabled student** you may qualify for a range of additional allowances to help with practical aspects of studying and any additional costs which your disability may cause you to incur. If, for example, you are visually impaired, you could apply for an allowance to pay for someone to read for you and assist in other tasks such as tracking down information in the library. You may also get funding for braille paper and audio-cassettes and other items of vital equipment. Students whose disability makes travelling to and from college more expensive can also apply for an additional travelling allowance.

☐ **If you have dependants** you may be able to claim an additional allowance. A husband, wife and children count as dependants, and you can also apply if you are a single parent.

☐ **Travelling expenses**: your grant automatically includes a specific amount for travelling (daily fares to college, plus the return fare home). However, if as part of your course you have to study or do some of your training in another part of the UK (if you're studying, say, medicine, nursing or dentistry, for instance) you can claim for the additional travel cost involved.

DISCRETIONARY GRANTS

If for some reason you have been denied a maintenance grant by your LEA you may qualify for a *discretionary grant*. To be honest, your chances of actually getting one are low, because the funds a LEA has available for providing discretionary grants are invariably very small, and the conditions you're required to satisfy are so restrictive as to put most students out of the running.

It's very difficult to give helpful guidelines because each individual LEA uses its own rules for deciding who qualifies for a discretionary grant. The best advice is to give it a go – and be pleasantly surprised if you succeed!

EARNING AND SAVING YOUR OWN MONEY

It's in your interest to build up some funds of your own before you arrive at college – especially as you may have to wait a few days – maybe as much as a couple of weeks – for your grant cheque to arrive, and then it has to be processed through your bank or building society account. There may be expenses even before you leave for college; deposits on a flat, for gas and electricity etc. Ideally, therefore, you should have a contingency fund of at least £400-£500 to ease you through any initial shortfalls or emergencies.

Set up your own college fund by opening the highest interest-earning building society account you can find. If you have a part-time job, try to put some money into the fund on a regular basis – even a small regular sum adds up appreciably over a few weeks and months. Add any gifts of money you receive. Christmas and birthdays are traditionally profitable occasions for raking in sizeable sums of money from relations (you may be able to up the amount by letting it drop that you're off to college in the near future). Do your best to resist the temptation to blow it all on a new CD player or whatever else is currently at the top of your 'must have' list. There'll come a time when you really appreciate having that money there to dip into.

> "My big mistake was not saving saving any of the money I earned during my year off before college. I blew it all travelling round Europe in the summer. My grant cheque arrived two weeks late and my parents couldn't afford to lend me enough money to tide me over. The hall of residence were good about my fee and let me pay when the cheque arrived. But you've still got to pay for food, books and bus fares. I got an overdraft in the end. I'd advise a new student to bring enough money to live on for at least a couple of weeks. You don't know your grant hasn't arrived until you get to college yourself."
>
> *First year student at Kingston University*

Save money by not paying tax unnecessarily

Earned income is taxable, but everyone can currently earn £3,445 a year (known as your personal allowance) before starting to pay tax. However, as a student you probably won't earn more than this in one year (your grant isn't counted as taxable income), even if you work full time throughout the summer vacation. When you start working, let your employer know you are a student and you won't have tax deducted from your earnings; you'll be asked to fill in Inland Revenue form P38(S). If by the end of the tax year (which runs from the 6th April to the 5th April) you find that your earnings have topped your personal allowance, you must declare them, but you'll only be required to pay tax on the excess.

You may be paying tax unnecessarily on savings in your building society account (or on your bank account if it's an interest-bearing one). Tax is levied on the interest, and deducted at source. If your combined job earnings and interest for a year come to less than your personal tax allowance of £3,445 a year, you can apply to have the interest on your savings paid without the tax being deducted. The building society or bank will have the appropriate form for you to complete.

BORROWING MONEY (1): A BANK OVERDRAFT

It's a financial fact of life that debt tends to snowball, so you'll be doing yourself an immense favour if you can avoid getting into it. However, not everyone who goes into the red has spent all their money on fags, booze and clubbing. An increasing number of students, for example, are suffering financial hardship because their parents aren't meeting their obligation to contribute to their grants.

So you could find that, however carefully you budget, you're going to have to supplement your grant by borrowing money. Don't feel a fiscal failure. An overdraft is a standard financial transaction, though best used sparingly because banks charge hefty arrangement fees and interest charges for the privilege.

However, as a student you have a useful card up your sleeve. Banks have changed drastically in recent years. Where once they offered customers a fairly basic service, they now go all out to sell what for them are highly lucrative financial *products*; insurance, pensions, mortgages, loans, sophisticated savings schemes et cetera.

As a future graduate you have, theoretically at least, great earnings potential. By getting their hooks into you now banks are gambling on having, in a few years' time, an identified, ready-made pool of customers ripe for these products. They call it investing in your future; cynics might regard it as a clever though somewhat risky marketing wheeze. Nevertheless, it'll probably be the one exception in your life to that well-known maxim: There's No Such Thing As A Free Lunch. You're under no obligation, moral or otherwise, to take up any of a bank's products after you graduate, at which time you can also move your account to a rival bank, should you choose to.

Arranging an overdraft facility

Arranging an overdraft is straightforward. All you have to do is make an appointment to see the *student manager* (each bank has a different title for the person responsible for handling student affairs). Explain to him/her what you want the overdraft for (it must be for a good reason – a payment from your parents being late rather than the sudden desire for a new camera), how you propose to repay it and how long it will take you to do so. It's important to be honest with the bank, and with yourself, about your ability to repay the money you borrow, especially if you're clocking up interest. Otherwise your debts simply continue to mount and the bank starts hassling you for real.

"The first time I went to see the bank about an overdraft I didn't sleep the night before! I'd hardly been inside a bank before, as I'd always used the cash dispenser outside. The man was quite friendly, and didn't treat me at all like an irresponsible idiot for getting into trouble. That's what had really been worrying me, because I'd been quite careful. He asked me a lot of questions, about why I had got into debt, what money I had coming in, that sort of thing."

Second year student at London University

When your application for an overdraft facility is accepted you'll be allowed to draw money up to an agreed amount, over an agreed period of time. Don't exceed this figure; if necessary, renegotiate the amount you need to borrow.

An overdraft facility isn't an automatic right. Financial etiquette requires that you get your bank's permission *before* you overdraw on your account. Don't think you can get away with being in the red for a few days without them noticing. They will – and you'll get a knuckle-rapping letter and, if you make a habit of such behaviour, a reputation for being financially irresponsible. This can be humiliating enough, but a bank also has the power to really punish you where it hurts: perversely, your already rapidly dwindling finances. A formally agreed overdraft on a student account will be interest-free up to a certain level (currently around £400), and then on amounts above this you'll be charged interest at a *preferential rate* (a lower rate than other, non-student, customers are charged).

However, go overdrawn without permission and you'll be charged a punitive rate (around 33%) for the entire quarter, the period over which banks calculate their charges. You may also lose your free banking concession, which means that your account will have hefty account handling and service charges deducted, as well as interest. Some banks charge a daily fee of several pounds to 'monitor' an account that's in trouble.

BORROWING MONEY (2): THE STUDENT LOAN

The student grant was frozen in 1990 (up until then it had increased annually roughly in line with inflation). Students are now 'encouraged' to take out a government-funded, non-means tested *Student Loan* to make up the shortfall.

You are eligible for a Student Loan if you are under the age of 50 when your course starts, a resident of the UK for the previous three years, and on a full-time higher education course lasting at least one year. You can apply for one Loan per academic year of up to £940 if you're studying at a London college and living in digs or college accommodation, £800 outside London, and £640 if you're living at home (1993/94 figures). Final year students receive less (£685, £585 and £470 respectively) as the Loan isn't intended to cover the summer break following finals.

You aren't expected to start repaying the Loan until after you graduate and are working in your first job. However, interest is charged on the Loan from the day the money enters your account. The interest rate, which is set annually in the late summer, is based on the Retail Price Index, and fluctuates according to inflation.

It's a waste of your resources to start paying interest charges until you have to. So before taking out a Student Loan, you should consider making use of your bank's interest-free overdraft facility.

When you can apply for a Student Loan

As soon as you get to college, or at any time during the academic year (the deadline is 31st July of the academic year for which you want the Loan). In other words, if you know right from the start that you're going to be short of money you can fill in the application form in the first week; or if you run into financial problems later on you can apply as and when you need to. It takes about 21 days for your application to be processed (although it can take longer if there's a flood of applications).

How to apply

You have to fill in three forms, which you obtain from your college. The first two forms, which your college initially processes, will decide whether you are eligible for a Student Loan. At this stage you need to show your birth or adoption certificate, your LEA award letter if you have one, and proof that you have a bank or building society account (ie your chequebook or passbook). Whichever type of account you have, it must be capable of receiving money by *electronic transfer*, as that's how your Loan will be paid.

The next step in the process is that your college will issue you with an *eligibility certificate* and an application form which you complete and send off to the Student Loan Company. The form asks you to supply two references, and state how much money you want to borrow. You can borrow any amount up to the limit (but if you borrow less than the limit you can't then apply for the remainder at a later date). You can also say whether you want the money in a lump sum, or divided into three instalments.

When the Student Loans Company receives your application you'll get back a formal loan agreement, plus a *direct debit mandate*. The mandate, which you give to your bank or building society, is an instruction to it to start repaying the loan in instalments after you graduate.

Repaying the Loan

You don't have to start repaying the Loan until the April after you graduate, although this can be deferred if you're unemployed or your earnings are less than 85% of the national average earnings. Repayments are monthly, and spread over five years if you're on a three or four year course, or seven years on a longer course.

BORROWING (3): FROM YOUR FAMILY

The major advantage of being able to borrow from your family is that your benefactor is unlikely to charge you interest on the loan, and may be much more flexible about when it's paid back (if at all).

Do use your judgement about who you approach, and how you go about it. A refusal is embarrassing to everyone concerned. If you know your parents are having problems making ends meet, it would be unfair to put them under even more pressure. Grandparents, on the other hand, may prove a better bet. If they've paid off their mortgage, for instance, they may have more money available to help you.

Bear in mind that students don't have the best reputation and that some people may not relish the prospect of supporting you through what they imagine to be three carefree years of drinking, smoking and generally living it up. Make it clear how important your studies are to you, and to your future career. Make it clear that you regard it as a loan, not a gift, and try and give a realistic date when you think you'll be able to repay it. Have a figure in mind. You'll sound more financially organised and responsible if you ask for a biggish sum (ie one that will help you through a term), rather than ask for £20 every now and again.

ACCESS AND HARDSHIP FUNDS

Every year the Department of Education and Science allocates special *Access funds* to all universities and colleges of higher education to provide additional help for students experiencing financial hardship. Some colleges also have their own special *hardship funds*, which are quite separate from the government-funded Access funds.

It's up to each individual college as to who receives a payment, and how much. Not surprisingly, as financial hardship becomes the norm for students, there is increasing pressure on what are very limited funds. So you need to act as soon as you know you need help, and to be able to put up a good case. Your college or student union welfare officer will help you with your application.

71

SPONSORSHIP

Getting your studies sponsored by a company or organisation could give your income a welcome boost, as well as provide opportunities for work during the vacation – not to mention the possibility of a job at the end of your three years. A large number of engineering students are sponsored, and other courses attracting the interest of sponsors include the sciences, business, accountancy and technology.

Dear Mr Sainsbury,

SPONSORSHIP

A sponsorship grant, or *bursary*, can be anything from £300 to £2,000 per year, and must be declared if you are also applying for a maintenance grant from your LEA. You're allowed £3,550 per year (1993/94 rates) before your sponsorship affects your grant, which will be reduced pound per pound above this amount.

What does the sponsor expect from you?

That depends on the individual company or organisation. If you are sponsored by one of the Armed Forces, you may be expected to undergo training during some of the vacations, and then to commit yourself to a period of service after your studies are completed. Some companies require you to work for them for a year before you start college, others during vacations or for a period after you graduate. If your course is a sandwich course, you may be paid a wage for the periods you spend on industrial placement with a sponsoring company, rather than receiving an annual grant.

When times are hard companies tend to be much more choosy about whom they sponsor, and they'll expect value for their money. You must be prepared to put a lot of work into tracking down the most appropriate sponsors for your particular interests – and then into convincing them you are worth sponsoring. The following publications give information on who is currently offering sponsorship schemes:

- *Sponsorship 1994*: This publication lists employers and professional bodies prepared to offer sponsorship for first degrees for courses beginning in 1994. Send a cheque or postal order for £3.56 payable to 'COIC' to Department CW, ISCO 5, The Paddock, Frizinghall, Bradford BD9 4HD.

- *A Question of Sponsorship?*: This is a free leaflet published by Student Sponsorship Information Services, obtainable from them by writing to PO Box 36, Newton-Le-Willows, Merseyside WA12 0DW.

- *The Which? Guide to Sponsorship in Higher Education* (published by Consumers' Association and Hodder and Stoughton).

CHARITIES AND EDUCATIONAL TRUST FUNDS

You may be able to get specific help with equipment, books, fees etc from a charity or an educational trust fund. Your local reference library will have publications listing participating organisations, including the following:

- *The Directory of Grant-Making Trusts* (published by the Charities Aid Foundation).

- *The Grant Register* (published by Macmillan Press).

- *Charities Digest* (published by the Family Welfare Association).

PART-TIME WORKING AT COLLEGE AND DURING VACATIONS

Not all that long ago you risked getting chucked out of college if you were caught working during term-time. Now university authorities realise that an increasing number of students have to do some sort of part-time job to make ends meet – especially when the alternative is dropping out of college altogether.

Part-time work is increasingly scarce – for the normal workforce as well as students – and what's available is likely to be poorly paid and at unsociable hours. Bear in mind that your first priority is your studies, so whatever you do shouldn't interfere with your work. Taking on nightshift work, for example, when you have 9am lectures is not a practical idea.

Even more important to consider is your personal safety, which could be put at risk if you are working late at night. Public transport will be scarce or more probably non-existent. Always make sure you can get home safely. Be very careful who you accept lifts from, and always have a few quid on you for a taxi in case of emergencies.

Act quickly and be imaginative when looking for work

Job vacancies go very quickly, so if possible, try and put some feelers out before you get to college. Many colleges and student unions run job vacancy lists, so contact your college/union to put your name down in the summer. You'll also get a head start on all the other students looking for work!

The campus itself can be a good source of work. Jobs in college canteens and the student union bar and shop are very popular and consequently get snapped up quickly. If you've got a place in a hall of residence you could try your hall canteen/dining room, which may take on students, and also the hall's administrative office.

Off-campus bars, pubs, restaurants, hotels and guest houses offer part-time shiftwork, and there are more opportunities for shiftwork in supermarkets, stores and shops, now that so many open in the evenings and all through the weekend.

The downside of this sort of work (apart from the unsocial hours and the poor pay) is that you'll be in competition with non-students as well. So instead of going for the obvious, take a good look at your own skills and accomplishments to see if one of those could prove a money-spinner. If you're good at languages, for example, you could try private coaching (you can advertise cheaply by putting up a card in your local newsagent). The same goes if you are proficient on a musical instrument – or at a sport. Football coaches are in demand by schools and local youth groups. Alternatively if you're a good swimmer in possession of a recognised lifesaving qualification you could find work at a local swimming pool or health club.

"Saturday jobs can restrict you, and you can't really do much at the weekend, or go home. A couple of evenings a week is about right – and if you work in the evenings you don't spend money! Bar work's the best. It doesn't pay the best, but it's socially good. You're not stuck out on your own in a completely foreign environment either. Our student union bar is pretty flexible. If you need the night off or you want to swap a shift they're fine about that."
Rachel Eccles, Town Planning student

If you have decent word-processing skills, you could try advertising on noticeboards round college – someone, somewhere, is bound to have a thesis, CV, academic paper or book they need typed up pristinely. If you get on with children, try advertising a baby-sitting service around college, starting with your own departmental lecturers (depending how cooperative your charges are, you may find it a good way to get some studying done). You could also consider advertising your services as a domestic cleaner or gardener.

Finding work for the vacation

Theoretically at least, the chances of finding a job for the vacation is more promising because you aren't so restricted in the number of hours you can offer a prospective employer (or when you are able to work), and seasonal work, when employers take on short-term workers, tends to coincide with university vacations.

Shops and stores traditionally take on extra staff at Christmas and sales times, for example. If you're studying in a town or city that attracts tourists in the summer (and often during Easter, too) there's often quite a range of casual work up for those who can grab it quickly. Pubs, restaurants, hotels big and small – even museums and theme parks – can be a good source of employment.

Many companies are keen to employ short-term workers as holiday relief for permanent employees. Sign on with a local employment agency (don't bother with the ones with the 'No Students' sign in the window), but make sure you do it well in advance of the vacation (again, you'll be competing with your fellow students). It's well worth building up a good relationship with an employer so that with any luck, you get regular vacation work out of them (if only on the basis of better the devil they know...).

There are also opportunities to work abroad in the long summer vacation, although just how successful a money-making exercise this can be is debatable as many students then splurge the money on seeing something of the country once their work is up. Typical jobs include hotel, bars and restaurants, fruit-picking and holiday repping, so you'll need at least a basic grasp of a language. Keep an eye out for advertisements in the quality newspapers in early spring and early summer, when holiday camping companies and American school camps advertise for summer help.

GETTING HELP FROM THE STATE

If you are a single student on a full-time course, you aren't eligible for *unemployment benefit* or *income support* during either term-time or more crucially, vacations, for the reason that you are not available for full-time work. However, if you are married (or co-habiting) you can apply for income support during the summer vacation, provided you and your partner are both students and bringing up a child.

If you are a disabled student, or a single parent responsible for bringing up a child under the age of 16, you may be eligible for income support during term-time and holidays. If you think you could be eligible for income support, contact your local Social Security office for an application form. Be aware that benefit rules are stringently, but not always accurately, applied. So if your applications is turned down by the DSS, never take no for an answer without speaking to your local Citizens' Advice Bureau.

If you're having trouble paying your rent, can you claim for housing benefit?

Unlikely, except under certain circumstances. You may be eligible for help if you and your partner are full-time students, especially if you have a child; if you are a single parent; if you are disabled. If you are already receiving income support you'll automatically be granted housing benefit.

If you are eligible for housing benefit, there are further conditions. If you are living in college-administered accommodation (a hall of residence or flat or house rented by the college) you will only get housing benefit for the summer vacations (ie not for during the term, or during Christmas or Easter holidays).

If, though, you are living in privately rented accommodation, you may be able to claim housing benefit during term and the three vacation periods. What you're allowed will depend on the actual rent, and you'll be expected to contribute to some of the cost yourself out of your grant (which, theoretically at least, includes provision for a roof of some sort over your head).

If you want to find out if you're entitled to housing benefit, contact your local council. Bear in mind that if you are granted housing benefit and you or your partner find part-time work during the term or vacation, you must inform the DSS and expect a pro rata reduction in your benefit.

TAKING A YEAR OFF TO HELP FINANCE YOUR STUDIES

At some time it may occur to you wonder if it's worth going to college at all if it means spending three or so years building up debts and several years thereafter struggling to pay them off. There's no doubt that a grant is woefully inadequate (even supposing you're lucky enough to be awarded a full one by your LEA), and that a sizeable and growing number of parents won't, or can't, contribute. For many students the solution is to borrow money, in the form of a Student Loan or an overdraft from a bank, and that's really little more than a euphemism for getting into debt.

There is an alternative, however, and that's taking a year off to work and save as much money as you can. Being able to support yourself through college – even if only for your first year – means putting off the moment you start borrowing money and consequently minimises your debts.

> "I took a year off solely to get some money together for college. I wished now that I had travelled, because I have ended up skint anyway!"
>
> *Nick Butcher,*
> *Media Studies student*

With jobs of almost any description being thin on the ground, you'll have to be prepared to put a lot of time and effort into securing work. Make use of your local Employment Office and register with employment agencies. Let everyone know that you're looking for a job (especially parents of your friends). Compile a list of local companies likely to be seeking staff and write to them, enclosing a CV detailing your educational qualifications, interests, previous work experience and any skills you may have. Increase your chances of getting work by doing a basic word-processing course. Be prepared to be offered the most basic and humdrum tasks (it's not as if you're going to have to do them for ever). Be enthusiastic and efficient and you could find yourself with a regular vacation job when you do start college.

Maximise your savings by putting them into the highest interest-earning account you can find. The type of account which requires you to leave your savings untouched for an agreed period (usually 3 months) offers a much better interest rate than the 'instant access' sort. It also protects you from the temptation to dip into your savings!

Chapter 6

FEEDING AND FENDING FOR YOURSELF

Cooking and eating facilities – learning to cook – healthy eating – where to go to buy food – comparing prices and getting value for money – basic kitchen equipment – basic ingredients – cooking terms and tips – hygiene and storing food – recycling – meals for your first week at college

Going away to university isn't just about studying for a degree. It's about learning to stand on your own two feet. That means taking responsibility for every facet of your life, from organising your finances to feeding yourself and running a home. So if you run out of clean underwear it's because you haven't got round to doing your washing this week. If there's nothing in the fridge it's because you forgot to pick something up on your way home. If the gas is cut off it's because you forgot to pay the bill.

That's the lecture out of the way. Going off to university and living away from home for the first time bring all manner of new challenges and responsibilities that it would be a wonder if you didn't feel a little overwhelmed – certainly for the first few weeks. You may also face situations and decisions you've never have had to deal with when living at home. Chapter 4 tells you how to deal with the money side of things on a day-to-day basis (budgeting, paying bills, dealing with the bank and so on). This chapter is all about handling the domestic side of your life.

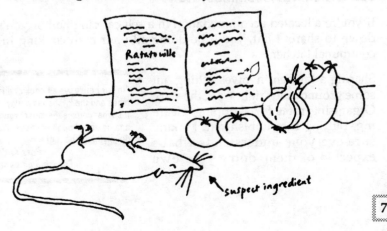

79

LIVING IN A HALL OF RESIDENCE

If you're lucky enough to be allocated a place in a hall of residence in your first year you won't have to concern yourself with tedious everyday chores such as remembering to pay bills and keeping the supply of toilet paper topped up. You may not have to do much cooking, either, if the hall has its own canteen for breakfasts and evening meals (although you may have to organise your evening meal on Sundays, when some halls provide lunch instead).

Even non-self-catering halls have a kitchen on each floor with basic facilities for making tea and coffee and a light snack. Expect at the most a kettle, a miniature oven (two rings and a small oven/grill) and an iron and ironing board. There may also be a small fridge – not that you'd be advised to risk leaving your precious food in it.

You'll need to buy your own personal supplies of tea, coffee, sugar, milk (long life or UHT if you don't have fridge facilities), biscuits, plus a small store of tinned baked beans and soup and some fruit. Never leave anything in the kitchen or it will disappear off the face of the earth — not that anyone will admit to 'borrowing' it! Keep all food in your room, along with your own mug, glass, plates and cutlery.

You'll be responsible for your own laundry (there'll be a laundry room in hall), and for keeping your own room tidy, although most halls have cleaners who do the basics like empty wastebins, change the sheets once a week, hoover and give the kitchen a quick flip over. You'll also be expected to clear up after yourself in the kitchen and bathroom.

SELF-CATERING ACCOMMODATION

If you're allocated accommodation in a self-catering hall or you're down to share a flat, you'll be doing all your own cooking in a communal kitchen.

Sharing a kitchen involves setting out some ground rules right from the start. Organising rotas for shopping, cleaning, putting the rubbish out. Making sure everyone understands what's expected of them, doing your own

"In our house we all cook at differe¦ times and the kitchen is always a ti¦ It's what causes the most argument¦ among us – though we never really do anything about it!"

Ross Anders¦
English Studies stude¦

share of the chores without prompting, and having a firm policy with slackers. Even the most motivated person will slip on occasion, though, perhaps because of the pressure of a looming essay deadline, so do make allowances.

It also saves time and money if you eat regular meals together, although how practical this is depends on your various commitments to college and leisure activities. This means sharing the cooking as well as the shopping. If one of the group hasn't cooked before, be encouraging; there's nothing more likely to put off an inexperienced chef than his or her flatmates taking the piss out of their efforts. If some one does prove to be irredeemably awful, do your palates a favour by letting the person in question opt out of cooking in exchange for taking on another responsibility.

DON'T WORRY IF YOU'VE NEVER COOKED BEFORE

If your culinary experience is limited to the occasional boiled egg or baked beans on toast, the prospect of cooking regular meals for yourself, let alone your flatmates, may fill you with apprehension. But don't worry. Hunger, and being used to decent home cooking, is the best possible spur to learning to cook.

> "I remember my first meal. I had a boil-in-the-bag and I managed to burn it!"
>
> Rachel Eccles,
> Town Planning student

And along the way, you may even discover just how satisfying and fun it can be. Anyone who's ever wielded a kitchen knife will tell you that there's something very therapeutic about peeling and chopping vegetables after a hard day's work. You'll also find that you're never without friends once you've acquired a reputation for providing 'a good table'.

If you are a novice cook, the food section of this chapter will give you all the basic information and techniques you need to shop for and cook your very first meal. The main thing is to keep your first attempts simple, and to help you on your way, there are seven easy-to-follow and inexpensive recipes to provide you with meals for a week.

When you're ready to extend your repertoire, you'll find the following cookbooks very useful – especially as they've all been written with the impecunious student in mind: *Grub on a Grant* by Cas Clarke (Headline, £4.99); *Cooking in a Bedsitter* by Katharine

Whitehorn (Penguin, £4.99); *Vegetarian Student* by Jenny Baker (Faber and Faber, £4.99); *The Student Cook Book* by Sarah Freeman (Collins and Brown, £4.99); *Students' Cookbook* by Sophie Grigson (Sainsburys, £1.95).

GAINING CONFIDENCE AND LEARNING TO IMPROVISE

When you first start cooking it's a good idea to follow a recipe exactly to the instructions, so you know what the dish is supposed to look and taste like. Then you can start adapting it to your own taste, adding a bit more of this, a little less of that, swapping one ingredient for another.

Before you know it, basic cooking techniques will become second nature, and you'll start gaining an instinct for what ingredients work well together, and what won't.

Pretty soon you'll have the confidence to start experimenting and improvising. This often starts by accident, when you realise one evening that there's hardly anything in the fridge or cupboard to make supper – but you manage nevertheless to knock up something really quite edible from the odds and ends you do have. That's when you begin to appreciate that doing your own thing is a large part of the fun of cooking.

HEALTHY EATING

To keep up the hectic pace at college you'll need a healthy diet that's varied enough to give you the right balance of starchy carbohydrates, fibre, protein, vitamins and minerals. Put simply this means eating plenty of the following:

- ❏ Potatoes, pasta, rice, wholemeal bread and cereals.
- ❏ Pulses such as lentils, kidney beans, chickpeas etc.
- ❏ Vegetables, fruit and nuts.
- ❏ Dairy products such as milk, eggs and cheese.
- ❏ Fish and lean meat such as chicken and turkey.

Keep your fat, sugar and salt intake low

These can be responsible for serious health problems later in life.

☐ Buy semi-skimmed or skimmed milk and low fat yogurts and cheese. Use margarines and cooking oils (eg sunflower, corn or rapeseed) that are high in polyunsaturates.

☐ When buying meat, choose the leanest you can afford. Cut off any fatty bits, and remove the skin (very high in fat) from chicken and turkey. Grill things like chicken, chops and sausages (lightly pricking the latter), as this lets the fat drain off. Dry-cook mince (ie without any additional oil) in a small frying pan and drain off the fat. Rather than fry hamburgers, bake them in the oven.

☐ Try to cut down on, or out altogether, sugar in your tea or coffee (or use sweeteners). Drink low calorie versions of fruit squashes and fizzy drinks like coke. Restrict your intake of cakes and biscuits, and use low-sugar jams, desserts, yogurts etc.

> "A lot of people eat badly, but I've never seen anybody undernourished."
> *Michael Poland,*
> *Applied Geology student*

☐ If you can't do without salt, use a low sodium brand such as Lo Salt. Taste food before automatically sprinkling on salt. Use herbs and spices to provide extra flavour.

Eating healthily as a vegetarian

Meat and fish are good sources of important things like protein, iron and the B vitamins, but vegetarians can get all of these from other foods. Leafy vegetables, for example, are rich in iron, while pulses, nuts and grains (rice, corn, wheat, rye etc), wholemeal bread and pasta and dairy products are excellent sources of protein. Textured vegetable protein made from soya beans (you can buy it in mince or chunk form) makes a useful and slightly chewy addition to savoury dishes (as does Quorn, although this is quite expensive).

WHERE TO GO TO BUY FOOD

You'll find it more convenient to shop near your home so you don't have to lug heavy bags of shopping long distances. Where exactly you shop depends on what's available locally.

> "If you do a weekly shop and eat loads of veg you can eat quite cheaply. It's just making the effort. If you just take a couple of of those pre-chilled meals off the supermarket shelf, or think sod it, I'll go and have a kebab, that all mounts up."
>
> *Andy Price, Estate Management student*

Provided you've got the storage space, it saves time and money if you can organise one big shop a week, rather than doing it in dribs and drabs. Most good quality vegetables and fruit (other than soft fruit) will last the week.

If you are fortunate enough to have reasonably sized freezer facilities, you can buy enough meat and fish to last the week, otherwise you'll have to shop for these items more or less as you need them, as they really only last for a couple of days when stored in the fridge.

Supermarkets

You'll find virtually everything you need, in a spacious, well-planned, albeit somewhat sterile environment. Wheeling up and down those long aisles can add significantly to your shopping time, though. Supermarkets reckon that fifty per cent of purchases in their stores are impulse buys, and to encourage this they carefully design their premises to lead you past shelves-full of tempting items you don't really need before you finally get to the basics you do. Shopping in a supermarket, therefore, requires a certain discipline, and you should always write out a full shopping list beforehand. If you share a flat, consider shopping in pairs to keep each other on the straight and

> "I have never really shopped or cooked for myself and it took about three months for me to get into some sort of routine."
>
> *Cheryl Allen, Law studen*

narrow. Remember that while the occasional impulse buy won't hurt too much, two or three such buys can take an appreciable chunk out of a tight budget. And don't shop when you're hungry – you always buy more!

The major advantage of shopping in supermarkets from your point of view is that because they have huge bargaining power, many items tend to be cheaper than at other places. Also, perishable products (meat, fish, bread, dairy products etc) are regularly and substantially reduced at the end of the day, especially on Saturdays, when they've reached their 'sell-by' date. You have to eat them within a couple of days, though, unless you can stick them in the freezer as soon as you get home. Another advantage of shopping in a supermarket is that you can choose your fruit and vegetables yourself, and you can buy as little (a single apple or carrot) or as much as you want.

Small/corner shops

Very handy, especially as they often stay open late. However, you pay for the convenience with higher prices, so keep your local shop for emergencies, like when you run out of milk or toilet paper.

Open air markets and stalls

Generally superb value for vegetables and fruit (and sometimes meat, fish and cheese as well), because they don't have anything like the running costs of shops. Quality can vary a bit, mostly because some unscrupulous stallholders will slip you second rate items without you knowing. Get to know which particular stalls offer the best quality and service. A word of caution: do not test fruit or vegetables by squeezing them – you'll get a volley of abuse.

Butchers and fish shops

Sadly fast disappearing from our high streets, but often a source of bargains. If you have one near you, look out for special offers on pre-packed mince, chicken and pork. Fish, although wonderfully nutritious, can be expensive, but mackerel and sardines in particular are a good buy.

Ethnic shops

If you have a Chinese, Indian, Greek, Cypriot or West Indian shop in your area, you're lucky. As well as usually carrying a small range of standard products, they're a marvellous source of herbs and spices, exotic fruit and vegetables, breads, sweetmeats, cheaply priced dried pulses and rice, and tinned and bottled products. And while supermarkets are now stocking an increasing range of ethnic products, you'll usually find them, or their even more authentic equivalents, cheaper in an ethnic shop.

Healthfood shops

Generally speaking, very expensive. Look for health/vegetarian foods and ingredients and environment-friendly cleaning products in supermarkets instead. Also, you can buy large 1kg packs of textured vegetable protein relatively cheaply from many ethnic shops.

COMPARING PRICES AND GETTING VALUE FOR YOUR MONEY

There's a knack to shopping to a tight budget, but it really boils down to keeping an eye open for a bargain and getting to know the prices of regular items on your shopping list. Make a practice of comparing the price of the same item across a range of brands, including the supermarket's own label version, and working out whether it would be better value to buy it in a bigger size, especially if it's something you buy regularly. Once upon a time this involved performing tortuous calculations in one's head, but many supermarkets are making life easier for the customer by providing a sticker on the edge of the shelf detailing each product/brand's price per 100 grams. But it's easy enough to work out that 80 teabags at 90p are better value than 40 teabags at 50p.

> "It works out cheaper if you do your shopping in a group, though it did tend to cause arguments about what everyone wanted to eat."
>
> *Simon, Humanities student*

- ❒ TV dinners and other ready-made meals may be very convenient (you just turn on the oven and stick them in), but they are far too expensive on your budget – apart from which if you enjoy a healthy appetite the portions aren't all that great. (Although by all means keep a couple in your freezer for emergencies and exam time.)

- ❒ Supermarkets' own label items are usually a few pence cheaper than their brand name equivalents. From time to time the major supermarkets also try to outdo each other with price wars on standard products such as baked

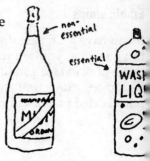

beans. If you have a choice of supermarkets locally, get into the habit of checking them out regularly so you can take advantage of the ensuing bargains.

❏ Buy packaged food (anything in bottles and tins) from supermarkets and fresh vegetables and fruit from markets and stalls.

❏ Most supermarkets have what's charmingly known in the trade as 'shit bins' – a shelf devoted to miscellaneous goods which have been reduced in price, perhaps because they are end of lines, the packaging has been damaged, or they're suddenly out of season (Easter eggs the week after Easter, that sort of thing). It's sod's law, of course, that there's rarely anything you actually want, but you could be lucky. Avoid buying dented tins (the contents may have deteriorated).

❏ Buy fruit and vegetables in season. Israeli-grown strawberries in the shops in January are very much more expensive than home grown berries in June.

BASIC KITCHEN EQUIPMENT

If you're allocated self-catering accommodation you'll be provided with basics like an oven and a fridge, and if you're *very* lucky a microwave oven and freezer facilities. Sometimes (but not often) there may even be cooking vessels and utensils, plus glasses, plates and dishes, cutlery and so on. However, you won't know the extent or state of what's available until you arrive, so it's probably wisest not expect too much and to take some things of your own. Besides, having your own things around helps make you feel more at home.

Basic kitchenware can be reasonably inexpensive, especially if you buy it from supermarkets and high street kitchenware shops. It can add up if you're buying several items though, so first ask your family (including aunts and uncles and grandparents) if they have anything they could donate. Most people have some doubles, not to mention sets of crockery that have been superseded by something more fashionable. They should be happy to help, especially if you use a little moral blackmail and imply that their donations will be crucial in ensuring you eat properly and regularly! Otherwise ask if you could have specific things as a Christmas or birthday present.

The most basic items you'll need in a kitchen

- [ ] *Kettle*
- [ ] *Tin opener* (buy a good one)
- [ ] *Corkscrew* and *bottle opener*
- [ ] *Cheese grater* (for pastas, pizzas etc)
- [ ] *Kitchen knives* (a bread knife, a vegetable knife and a larger bladed knife for cutting/carving meat)
- [ ] *Wooden spoon* (for stirring)
- [ ] *Ladle* (for serving soup, stews, sauces etc)
- [ ] *Slatted spatula* (for stir-frying, dishing up hamburgers, fried eggs etc)
- [ ] *Potato masher*
- [ ] *Measuring spoons* (ie a tablespoon and teaspoon – useful as an alternative way to measure ingredients if you don't have weighing scales or plastic measuring cups)
- [ ] *Sieve* (a metal one is more durable than a plastic one)
- [ ] *Chopping board*
- [ ] *Bowls* (for mixing ingredients and for serving salads, vegetables etc)
- [ ] *A couple of plastic containers with lids* (for storing leftovers in the fridge)
- [ ] *Frying pan*
- [ ] *3 saucepans* (one small, one medium and one large enough for cooking things like pasta)
- [ ] *Medium-sized ovenproof casserole dish* (for stews and pasta dishes etc baked in the oven; also doubles up as a serving dish)
- [ ] *Roasting tin* (for roasting meat, baking hamburgers, potatoes etc)
- [ ] *Shallow oven dish* (for baking vegetables, pies etc, also doubles up as a serving dish)

PLUS *plates, soup/cereal bowls, a mug and a glass, a set of cutlery.*

Equipment you'll also find useful to have as and when you can acquire it

☐ *Garlic press*

☐ *Wooden rolling pin*

☐ *Balloon-shaped egg whisk*

☐ *Electric food blender or processor* (speeds up tedious cooking tasks like grating and shredding, mixing, pureeing etc)

☐ A set of *weighing scales* or a set of *plastic measuring cups*

☐ *Stainless steel colander* (for draining and steaming vegetables)

☐ *Kitchen scissors*

☐ *A measuring jug* (you can use a pint or half pint beer mug as an alternative)

☐ *Pressure cooker* (reduces cooking time to a fraction, and very useful for cooking dried pulses and stews)

☐ *Simple knife sharpener* (makes cutting and chopping vegetables and meat much easier)

☐ *A microwave oven*

BASIC COOKING INGREDIENTS

Agree with your flatmates what meals you'll be sharing on a regular basis and the type of foods you like. This will give you an idea of the basic items your weekly shopping trip and the food kitty will cover. (Note that expensive or obscure tastes are the responsibility of the individual concerned and shouldn't be funded out of the general kitty.) Keep a running list for people to make a note of items that are due to run out. As a basic principle, the person who uses the last of the milk, toilet paper or other crucial items is responsible for replacing them as soon as possible.

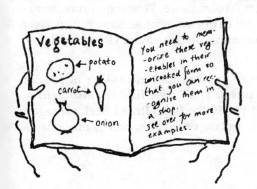

You should also aim to build up a small stock cupboard so you always have the basic ingredients for knocking up a meal or snack. Add two or three items a week – a couple of extra tins of beans and other vegetables, some pasta and rice etc. Similarly you'll want to build up a small collection of dried herbs and spices for using in different sorts of dishes. These can be quite expensive, so start off with the ones you'll use most often (ie mixed herbs, oregano, chilli or curry powder) and add a new herb or spice each week.

Staples to always have in the house:

Milk, coffee, tea, sugar, biscuits, bread, breakfast cereals, tinned soups, vegetable oil for cooking, margarine, jam, peanut butter.

You'll find the majority of your meals will be based on: Pasta, rice or potatoes.

Choosing one of these three as your basis, you can create a simple, nourishing and inexpensive meal by adding one or more of the following ingredients:

- ❒ Inexpensive cuts of meat or fish
- ❒ Tinned meat (ie corned beef, hot dogs) or fish (tuna, sardines)
- ❒ Beans (baked beans, chickpeas, peas, lentils, kidney beans etc. Beans are a cheap and nourishing way of bulking out a meal)
- ❒ Eggs and cheese
- ❒ Tinned, frozen or fresh vegetables (always keep a supply of onions and tinned tomatoes)

Add flavour to a dish with one or more of the following: Salt and pepper; herbs and spices; garlic; tomato puree; white or red wine vinegar; bottled table sauces (brown sauce, Worcester sauce, tomato ketchup etc) and relishes; Parmesan cheese; soya sauce; West Indian or Malaysian pepper sauces; Indian chutneys and Vindaloo, Madras and Tikka pastes.

If you have freezer facilities you can take advantage of special offers on meat in supermarkets. You'll also find it convenient to keep a supply of some of the following: Minced beef, sausages, chops, semi-skimmed milk, frozen vegetables, bread, pizza bases etc.

BASIC COOKING TIPS

Anyone interested in learning to cook needs a good basic cookbook such as *Delia Smith's Complete Illustrated Cookery Course* or the *Good Housekeeping Cook Book*. As well as having literally hundreds of wide-ranging recipes, such books will provide a useful reference on cooking terms and techniques. It's well worth splashing out on a general cookbook – or even better, dropping a few hints at home about what a good 'off to college'/birthday/ Christmas present one would make!

> 'Start eating lots of rice and pasta and spuds. It can get boring, but t's cheap. Try to avoid McDonalds, which isn't!"
>
> Nick Butcher,
> *Media Studies student*

In the meantime, though, here are a few immediate questions that might crop up in your initial attempts at cooking.

How can you measure ingredients if you don't have scales?

A quick glance through any recipe shows that measurements are used to give the right amount of a particular ingredient. However, it's perfectly possible to cook without using scales, by, for example, using something else like a tablespoon or teaspoon or a pint or half pint glass.

Often a recipe will state, say, a 375g tin of tomatoes or kidney beans – in which case you just chuck in the whole contents of the tin. Meats and cheeses are often sold prepacked with the weight stated on the packaging, so you can either buy the exact quantity you require or use the weight stated as a guide to cut the appropriate portion. You can also buy vegetables in specific amounts, but to be honest, a few extra carrots or potatoes isn't going to harm a dish.

What will spoil it though, is adding too much salt or hot spice. Even too many herbs can overwhelm a dish. It's very much a matter of personal taste how spicy or salty you like your food (although do bear in mind your fellow flatmates' preferences if you're cooking for them as well). Always start by adding salt, herbs, spices and anything hot in tiny quantities. Taste the food and then add a little more if you think it needs it.

NB: You'll notice that a recipe usually gives quantities in both imperial (pounds and ounces) and metric (grams and kilograms) measurements. Stick to one or the other, never mixing the two. Recipes are increasingly following the American method of giving quantities in $1/4$, $1/2$ or 1 cup measurements (especially useful for measuring flour, sugar etc). You can buy a cheap set of plastic measuring cups from supermarkets and high street cookware shops.

Has a dish cooked long enough?

Recipes always say how long a particular dish needs to cook, and manufacturers give recommended cooking times on their packaging. However, cooking times can vary from oven to oven, and from gas to electricity, so you should always test a dish when it's just about ready and make your own decision. (A little bit of experience with your oven will soon give you an idea which side it errs on.)

Some foods (stews and casseroles) are improved by cooking a little longer, and cheaper cuts of meats benefit from long and slow cooking so that they're not tough. With other foods (grilled or poached fish) the timing is more critical; vegetables become mushy and not especially nice if over boiled, and they lose most of their vitamins.

Pasta shouldn't be overcooked either. Check a strand or piece when it's just about ready. If it's cooked it should be what's called *al dente* – just firm enough to give a slight resistance when you bite into it.

It's a matter of personal taste whether you prefer roast beef, steak or lamb (if you can afford them) on the rare side, but there are some meats, pork but particularly chicken and turkey, which must be cooked fully to kill off any salmonella bacteria they may be harbouring. If in doubt, cut into the centre of a pork chop and give it a bit longer under the grill if it looks pink. With chicken or turkey, stick the point of a sharp knife into the thickest area – if either the flesh or the juices that run out look a little pink, give it a few minutes longer. If chops, sausages or chicken joints look as though they're burning or cooking too quickly under the grill, turn the heat down, and turn the meat every few minutes.

What should you do with leftovers?

Never throw them out, for a start. Leftovers are one of the great unsung joys of cooking, yet it's surprising how many people chuck them in the bin. Apart from the moral aspect of throwing out food, on your budget you can't afford to waste any.

Cool the leftover food, cover it with a lid or some cling film and put in the fridge. You can use it within the next two or three days, but reheat it thoroughly to get rid of any potentially harmful bacteria. Pastas, stews and casseroles, rice dishes, chilli-con-carne, pizzas etc are wonderful (sometimes even better) the next day. Vegetables can be combined and reheated in some oil in a frying pan to make delicious bubble and squeak, added to stews, pies and casseroles, or used as the basis of a delicious, nourishing, quick to make and extremely cheap soup (chop them up and put in a saucepan, add some water, seasoning and as an optional extra a can of soup or beans. Simmer over a medium heat for a few minutes).

HYGIENE AND STORING AND HANDLING FOOD

Food poisoning is reported on the increase, due, it's thought, to bad kitchen hygiene and poor food handling. So to a large extent it's preventable.

The bacteria that cause food poisoning thrive on the warm, moist and potentially dirty conditions a kitchen has to offer. (Crumbs and spilled food also encourage mice and insects). It's important, therefore, to set up a rota with your flatmates to keep your kitchen clean and tidy, and to follow a few basic rules when storing and handling food.

❑ **Washing up should be done regularly, worktops wiped, floors swept and washed.** Mop up spills immediately, especially on the floor where they could cause an accident. Empty your kitchen rubbish bin regularly.

❑ **Wash your hands before preparing food**, and particularly after handling raw meat. Wash your chopping board, knives and any other equipment after preparing raw food. Change tea towels regularly and dry thoroughly after use.

☐ **Keep meat, dairy products, bread, eggs and leftovers in the fridge.** Everything should be stored wrapped or covered to prevent cross contamination of bacteria, and also of smell. Don't keep half-used tins in the fridge. The taste of the metal can contaminate the contents, so transfer them to another container. Cool hot dishes to room temperature before refrigerating. Raw meat should be stored in the bottom of the fridge to prevent drips contaminating other cooked or ready to-eat food. If your fridge isn't self-defrosting, you'll need to do this yourself regularly, depending on how quickly the ice builds up, otherwise the fridge won't work efficiently.

☐ **Food left out of the fridge** (ie something you're cooling or defrosting) should be covered. If you keep fruit in a fruit bowl wash things like apples before eating them (especially important in summer when flies are around).

☐ **Thaw out all frozen foods, especially poultry, thoroughly before cooking** (unless the instructions specifically say you can put a frozen item straight into the oven or microwave). Once something has been defrosted, do not refreeze it. You can, though, thaw meat, cook it and freeze the resulting dish.

☐ **Don't use food that's way beyond the 'sell by' date stamp on the pack, tin or jar.** It's likely to have deteriorated in quality, and may even be harmful. If something in your fridge is off you can usually tell by the smell; discolouration can also be a clue (although fresh mince and other red meat can go a slightly grey colour after a day in the fridge – a natural and harmless effect of oxidation). It's better to be safe than violently throwing up, so if in doubt, throw it out.

RECYCLING

Do your bit for the environment by recycling glass bottles and jars, newspapers and magazines and aluminium cans. It really does help cut down on waste and energy (every tin can produced in the UK contains about 20% of recycled material). An increasing number of supermarkets have recycling facilities outside their stores to help you do this. Most local councils have recycling centres, although it means transporting the stuff there yourself. If you don't have access to a car, your council may have a collection service.

Wherever you can, buy things like stationery, files etc made from recycled paper or board (major high street stationers carry a complete range). Save plastic carrier bags to use again when you go shopping.

SEVEN MAIN MEALS FOR THE WEEK

Much of your first week will be spent dashing from one freshers event to another, so you'll probably be eating in the college canteen for a lot of the time. When you do get round to cooking at home (sharing a meal is a great way of getting to know your new flatmates) you might find yourself wondering what on earth to cook.

The seven following main meals are straightforward and easy to make, even if you're a complete novice. All (apart from the hamburgers) can be vegetarian by adjusting one or two or the ingredients. You can repeat them on a weekly cycle for several weeks – until you finally get bored enough to want to add something new to the repertoire!

SPAGHETTI BOLOGNAISE   *(Feeds 4)*

2-3 tablespoons of vegetable oil
2 medium onions, chopped
2-3 cloves of garlic, finely chopped (optional)
1lb minced beef
2 teaspoons dried oregano
2 tablespoons of tomato puree
1 379g tin of tomatoes
$^{3}/_{4}$ pint of water
A 1lb pack of quickly cooking spaghetti (or other pasta)

1. Heat the oil in a heavy based saucepan, add the onions and garlic and cook together for about 5 minutes until soft.

2. In a separate saucepan or frying pan, dry-cook the mince on a low heat for about 5 minutes and then drain off the fat. Stir the mince into the onions and garlic.

3. Add the oregano, tomato puree and tinned tomatoes (chopping up the tomatoes in the saucepan). Stir in the water, and then simmer the sauce on a low heat for at least half an hour (the longer, the better). Stir occasionally, adding a bit more water if the sauce starts getting dry.

4. In a separate saucepan, boil plenty of water (takes about 5 minutes) and then add the pasta. Separate the strands using a fork and cook the pasta for the time specified on the pack. Test a strand to check it's ready. Drain.

5. Serve the pasta in individual bowls or plates and top with the sauce. People can season with salt, pepper and ready-grated Parmesan cheese for themselves.

Leftover appeal: Excellent heated up (in a little oil) the next day.

Vegetarian variation: Substitute the mince for a soya protein mince or some sliced mushrooms, courgettes or broccoli instead. The cooking time will be much shorter.

Chilli con carne: You can use the sauce as the basis of a chilli, adding two tins of kidney beans towards the end of the cooking time, and a couple of teaspoons of chilli powder or chop 3 hot dried peppers to give it a little kick. Serve with rice instead of pasta.

LEEK AND POTATO PIE

(Feeds 4)

> 4 medium-sized leeks
> 2 large onions
> 2lb potatoes
> $^1/_2$ lb smoked streaky bacon
> 2 tablespoons vegetable oil
> 5fl oz single cream (optional)
> Pepper to season
> 2 teaspoons dried mixed herbs

1. Preheat the oven to Gas Mark 7/220°C/425°F.

2. Peel and boil the potatoes until cooked. Drain (keeping the potato water) and slice reasonably thinly.

3. De-rind and cut bacon into thin strips. Peel and roughly chop the onions. Top and tail leeks, remove outer layer, slice into $^1/_2$" pieces and rinse thoroughly.

4. Heat the oil in a frying pan on a low heat and gently fry together the leeks, onion and bacon for about 10 minutes, until everything's soft but not brown.

5. Layer the leek mixture and the potatoes in a medium-sized ovenproof dish. Start with the potatoes, covering the bottom of the dish, and sprinkle a little pepper and some herbs. You should have two layers of leek mixture and a topping of potatoes. Gently pour over enough potato water to just about reach the top layer of potatoes. Sprinkle the rest of the herbs on top.

6. Place in the oven and cook for approximately 40 minutes. Remove from the oven and pour the cream over the dish, giving it a gentle shake to help the cream drizzle down. return to the oven for another 10 minutes. Serve with a vegetable of your choice.

> *Leftover appeal: Excellent. Heat up in some oil or use as the basis of a homemade soup.*

Vegetarian variation: Omit the bacon and add 1 level teaspoon of salt and some extra herbs for flavour. You can also grate some Cheddar cheese on each leek and onion layer, and on to the top of the dish.

MINCE, VEGETABLE AND POTATO PIE   *(Feeds 4)*

$^3/_4$ lb minced beef
2 medium onions, roughly chopped
2 tablespoons vegetable oil
1 tin chickpeas
2 large carrots, peeled and chopped into smallish pieces
Any other left-over vegetables from the fridge
5-6 medium-sized potatoes
2 teaspoons dried mixed herbs
1 large tablespoon tomato puree
A generous dash of bottled brown sauce
$^1/_2$ pt water

1. Preheat the oven to Gas Mark 7/220°C/425°F.

2. Peel and boil the potatoes until just cooked. Drain and slice reasonably thinly.

3. Gently dry-cook the mince on its own for a few minutes, and drain off the resulting fat. Heat the oil in a frying pan or deep saucepan over a low heat. Add the onions and carrots and cook for 5 minutes until the onions are soft. Add the mince, herbs, chickpeas, leftover vegetables, brown sauce and puree. Stir in the water, and let the mixture simmer for about 15-20 minutes.

4. Transfer the mixture to a casserole or other ovenproof dish, and layer the sliced potatoes on the top. Sprinkle with a few herbs and transfer to the oven for approximately 30 minutes, or until the potatoes look browned and crispy. Serve with a green vegetable.

Leftover appeal: Excellent. Reheat in a little oil.

Vegetarian variation: Substitute the minced beef for a soya protein mince, or some more beans and vegetables.

PIZZA

(Feeds 1)

A most filling and nutritious meal, and easy to make yourself. You're only limited by your imagination – and how much you can pile on! The classic cheese used is Mozzarella, but Cheddar is a much cheaper alternative and just as tasty. You can buy a pizza-base mix, but it's quicker and less fiddly to buy the ready-made bases, or use a chunk of a french loaf split in half.

One ready-made base
One medium-sized onion, finely sliced and gently fried
4 medium-sized mushrooms, washed and thinly sliced
3-4oz grated Cheddar cheese
$^1/_2$ tin tomatoes (the juice drained off)
$^1/_2$ green pepper, thinly sliced
A generous sprinkling of dried oregano and/or basil

Alternative toppings:

Ham, salami, pepperoni, sausages, corn, tuna, olives, anchovies, slices of fresh tomatoes, pineapple chunks, chopped chilli peppers.

1. Preheat the oven to Gas Mark 4/180°C/350°F.

2. Assemble the pizza, starting with a layer of tomato, then the onions, green pepper, mushrooms, cheese and finally the herbs.

3. Carefully place in the oven (you can put it straight on the shelf) and cook for 10-15 minutes, until the cheese has melted. Serve with a salad.

Leftover appeal: *Excellent cold the next day. If the base has gone a bit soggy, stick it in the oven for a few minutes.*

KEBABS

(Feeds 2 people.
Allow one 9" stick per person)

You can buy inexpensive metal skewers from supermarkets or cookware shops. Pork, sausages or hotdogs are the cheapest meat to use; chicken and lamb are also suitable, but more expensive.)

$3/4$ lb pork or chicken, cut into $1^1/_2$" cubes
1 medium-sized onion, peeled and quartered
1 green pepper, cut into large ($1^1/_2$" square) sections
$1/4$ lb mushrooms, washed
1 tomato, halved (optional)

1. Thread the meat, onion, pepper, mushrooms and tomatoes alternately on to the stick. Place on the grill pan and grill at a medium heat for about 20 minutes, turning so that all sides are done. The meat must be properly cooked, so if the vegetables look as though they're doing too quickly, turn the heat down (though a little charcoal gives them flavour).

2. Serve with a salad, plus some sautéd potatoes or rice.

To sauté potatoes: Boil some potatoes until they're cooked. Slice thickly and gently fry in some oil in a frying pan until crisp and brown (takes about 10 minutes).

You can liven up the rice by: Cooking it according to the instructions on the packet, draining, and adding a combination of some of the following: cooked peas, tinned corn, chopped spring onions or lightly fried ordinary onions, a chopped up boiled egg, bean shoots, mushrooms – or anything else available. Season with plenty of salt and pepper and a generous splash of soya sauce.

Vegetarian variation: Substitute the meat with prawns if you're a fish eater, or other chunky vegetables such as courgettes, aubergines and bananas.

CHEESY PASTA   (Feeds 4)

Three quarters of a bag of penne or other chunky pasta
$1/_2$ lb smoked steaky bacon, de-rinded & cut into thin strips
1 large onion, finely chopped
$1/_4$ lb mushrooms, sliced
$1/_2$ lb broccoli (or one medium head)
1 379g tin tomatoes
2 tablespoons vegetable oil
6oz grated Cheddar cheese
2 heaped teaspoons dried oregano
1 mixed teaspoon dried basil

1. Preheat the oven to Gas Mark 6/200°C/400°F.

2. Cook the pasta in boiling water for 10 minutes and drain.

3. Cut the broccoli into bite-sized chunks, cook briefly in boiling water for 3-4 minutes, and drain.

4. Gently fry the oil, bacon and onions in a frying pan for about 8 minutes. Add the tomatoes, gently mashing them, herbs and finally the cheese. Cook gently until the cheese has melted.

5. Using the largest casserole or ovenproof dish you have, combine the pasta, broccoli, mushrooms and the sauce, mixing everything up well. Sprinkle some additional cheese and herbs on top and cook in the middle of the oven for about 15 minutes. The top should be golden and a bit crispy when you take it out.

> **Leftover appeal:** *If anything, even better reheated the next day.*

Vegetarian variation: Omit the bacon, and use a rennet-free Cheddar if you're a strict vegetarian. The dish also works well with courgettes.

HAMBURGERS

(Feeds 2)

Homemade hamburgers are inexpensive, easy to make and vastly superior to anything you can buy in the high street. If you want to make the meat go further, add some breadcrumbs to the mixture.

> 1lb minced beef
> 1 medium onion, finely chopped
> 2 teaspoons dried mixed herbs

1. Preheat the oven to Gas Mark 7/220°C/425°F).

2. In a large bowl, mix well the mince, onion and herbs. Mould into four hamburgers, flatten slightly, and sprinkle a few extra herbs on top. Put in a cooking tin and cook in the middle of the oven for approximately 20 minutes.

3. Serve with or without hamburger baps, accompanied by mashed or sautéd potatoes, baked beans or peas and a relish of your choice.

4. When it's in season, corn-on-the-cob is great with hamburgers. Remove outer leaves and silky strands and cook in boiling water for about 12 minutes. Drain and serve with a knob of butter and plenty of pepper.

Chapter 7

GETTING DOWN TO WORK

Self motivation – getting a study routine going – buying books and equipment – lectures, seminars and tutorials – using the library – study techniques – coping with revision and exams

Once the mad, exciting whirl of Freshers Week is over, it's time to work. Don't expect any gentle lead-in, either. There's a lot of work to get through in the term, and you'll be expected to get into the swing of lectures, tutorials, libraries, personal studying and so on right from the word go.

For many new undergraduates the biggest surprise is not so much the amount of work but the freedom you're given in which to accomplish it – or not, as the case may be. You'll really notice the difference if your A Level studies were fairly closely supervised by teachers, and the bulk of your days were spent on the school premises. At university you'll be left much more to your own devices, responsible for organising and keeping on top of your work, handing in essays and laboratory projects on schedule and getting the necessary readings done in time for lectures and seminars. And if you don't have reason to go into college on a particular day, you can stay at home and suit yourself how you spend the time.

You could coast along quite nicely – but not for very long. You'll be assessed at various stages throughout the year, through coursework as well as end-of-term/year exams. Not only do your results determine the length of your university career (you'll be booted out if you don't come up to scratch), but they may also count towards the final classification of degree that you receive at the end of it all.

Studying for a degree is very different to studying for A Levels in other ways. You delve into, pick over and analyse a subject in much greater depth than you'll have ever done before. In the process you're expected to come up with your own ideas, interpretations and evaluations. You're expected to think for yourself, not regurgitate the opinions of others. You can only do this if you get involved with your subject from day one.

WHAT DO YOU WANT FROM THREE YEARS AT UNIVERSITY?

This is a question you should ask yourself before you even set foot in your first lecture hall. Your answer will help you establish your motivation, and therefore how much effort you want to put into your studies.

University isn't just about graduating with a Triple First after three years of intensive studying, although if that's your aim, good luck. University is also about broadening your experiences and your perspective on life through learning to become independent, meeting new people and making the most of experiences and opportunities that weren't available to you back at home. If, during your time, you've made the most of everything university has to offer, you'll emerge a more rounded, maturer person with well-developed social and intellectual skills. The perfect basis for the next stage in your life; getting that all important first job.

To really make the most of university you have to get the balance right between work and pleasure, and that means managing your study time so that you have adequate time for social and leisure activities. Any future employer will expect you first and foremost to be a flexible, well-rounded person, capable of getting on with colleagues and doing things the corporate way. Someone who has spent three years studying to the exclusion of everything else might not (rightly or wrongly) be perceived as 'company material'.

Even if your aim is to combine three years of fun with obtaining a reasonable if unexceptional degree, you will still need to study consistently. If you've chosen a vocational course such as law, engineering or medicine then obviously the standard of your work and ultimately your degree are crucial to your chances of becoming a lawyer, engineer or doctor.

It's a similar situation if you want to carry on studying as a post-graduate. You'll require a grant to finance your further studies, and grants, being few and far between, are highly competitive. If you graduate with anything less than an Upper Second (2:1) you haven't a chance of getting one, and even then you'd be advised to aim for a First. The problem is that you may not actually realise you want to do postgraduate studies until your final year, by which time you will need had to have demonstrated a record of excellent grades for essays, dissertations, laboratory projects and exams.

ORGANISING YOUR STUDY TIME

When you receive your first timetable and see those huge blocks of 'free' time between lectures and tutorials it's tempting to think there's masses of time to do your personal studying. In fact, the opposite is true. The more time you think you have to get a job done, the longer you put it off until it inevitably becomes a last minute, burning-the-midnight-oil affair. Because you're not focusing your time and your efforts, you spend far more time than the job deserves, time you could be using more profitably.

Organising your studies so that you get a routine going means you spend *less* time working and more time having fun, because you know what you've got to do and you've put aside the appropriate time to get the job done. If you're in the habit of working for a couple of hours when you get back from your afternoon lectures you're not so likely to switch on the TV or allow yourself to get sidetracked by your flatmate or nextdoor neighbour. A good routine also becomes automatic and has a momentum of its own; if your two hours after college is interrupted you're more likely to feel dissatisfied than relieved.

How do you find out what is the best routine for you? Expect a bit of trial and error to begin with, but your routine shouldn't be so inflexible and demanding that sticking to it is a real effort. That defeats the whole purpose. It will be structured around your lecture and tutorial timetable, your part-time job and any scheduled leisure or sporting activity. Personal studies (reading, researching and writing essays and dissertations etc) have to be slotted in the remaining time – such as it may be. Now you know why it's so important to be organised.

It's easier to study some times than others

Although some aspects of your day are set in stone, you'll find your personal study periods will be more productive if you can schedule them, as far as is practical, around the time of the day you're at your most receptive. We all have times of the day when we feel particularly alert, and times when we feel lethargic. You may find, for instance, that you can get an enormous amount of work done in the two hours before breakfast. Your mind is fresh after a good night's sleep and it's so early there are few distractions to interrupt your concentration. You may even find that you get a second wind in the evening after supper. It's important, though, to allow yourself some time to wind down between finishing work and going to bed.

Early afternoons, on the other hand, could be an entirely different matter. It's a time for many people when their energy levels take a dive. Do you find a couple of pages of turgid text have you nodding off? If so, it doesn't matter how much you struggle to maintain your concentration, you're not going to get much effective studying done, which can be discouraging, especially if you're grappling with a tricky topic. It's far wiser to (a) admit your limitations and plan to use the time more effectively in another way, or (b) extend your morning work period until 1.30-2pm, especially if that's when you normally do your best work, and take your lunch break during your 'down' period.

YOUR ENVIRONMENT IS IMPORTANT

Just as important as when you study are the conditions you work in. If there's something about them that's not quite right it's another thing to affect your concentration and your sense of control over your work. If possible, work at a desk or table, with a hardback chair to support your back. Working on your bed can be a little too relaxing, apart from giving you cricks in various parts of your body.

Try also to keep your immediate surroundings reasonably neat and tidy. Have on your desk before you such materials you need for the specific task in hand. Lots of clutter is distracting – and reminds you of all the other work you still have to do.

You should also be warm and comfortable – but the room shouldn't be too hot and stuffy or you'll be forever dropping off. Have a window open to let in fresh air (especially if you smoke). In winter, open the window once in a while to give your room a quick, refreshing burst of air. If you're living in a hall of residence you'll won't find being cold too much of a problem, as student rooms have central heating and sometimes a small electric wall heater (usually coin-operated) to supplement the heat. Another, even bigger advantage, is that your heating bills are already accounted for in the hall fees you pay at the beginning of each term, so you won't have to worry about whether you can afford to keep a radiator on.

If you're living in lodgings or sharing a flat, though, the situation could be altogether different – not to mention chillier. Heating is often inadequate and, if you've got night storage heating, the one thing you can be sure of is that it will never be on when you really need it. You could consider clubbing together with your flatmates to buy an electric or fan heater for the main living area, but it isn't particularly cheap to run. In really cold weather you're better off studying in the college library, or even in bed with a hot water-bottle.

BOOKS: TO BUY OR NOT TO BUY?

If there's one thing that really exasperates all students without exception, it's being handed a long list of books to buy at the beginning of term, dutifully shelling out £100 or more – and then finding they're of no real use to the course.

Theoretically the grant/Student-Loan is supposed to include an allowance for books, but you'd be forgiven for thinking the bright spark who set the amount had never been near a book shop in his or her life. Academic textbooks are extremely expensive – ranging from £7 or £8 to as much as £25 – and that's only for a paperback!

The summer reading list

Some universities send a reading list to new students in the summer holidays, the idea being that by reading a few of the suggested books (you don't have to read them all, unless you choose to) you have a basic familiarity with the subject by the time you arrive at college. A good idea, too – except you should resist the temptation to buy any of the books on the list. It's likely that most of the suggestions will be for background reading only ('phone up and check with the department). Far better to save your money for books you really need at college and borrow from your local library.

Find out which books are crucial to your course

You're going to have to be very selective in the books you buy because you'll only be able to afford a few. Ask lecturers for each of your individual courses which books are *really* important. A book you're going to refer to again and again is worth owning. A book from which you only take one reading is not. Think twice about any book a lecturer highly recommends if he or she is the author – if necessary, ask the lecturer to justify why his/her book is so crucial to your understanding that it's worth you spending the equivalent of two weeks' food on it.

You can save money on books by clubbing together with a couple of other people on your course and sharing. Keep an eye out too for secondhand copies from second and third year students (check out your department or commonroom notice board), college or student union book sales and second hand bookshops (which usually abound in university towns). If it's important that the information is bang up to date (which may be in the case of scientific or medical theory), make sure any secondhand book you buy is a recent enough edition.

Your college library will also be a rich source of reference books, but with the disadvantage that forty or more of you could be chasing the same book in the same two day period. Again, if it's that crucial and it's still in print, it might be worth clubbing together to buy your own copy – or alternatively to buy photostats as and when you need them. If there's a municipal library near to college or your lodgings it's worth joining. It may not have the more specialist books and periodicals you need, but there's bound to be a selection of more general books available (literature, business etc).

EQUIPPING YOURSELF FOR YOUR STUDIES

You'll be expected to provide your own stationery, which will include A4-sized files (at least one per course), A4 paper (blank, lined, graphed as appropriate), pens, pencils and other necessary writing and drawing equipment. Look out for bargains in the annual back to school or college promotions run by most high street stationers in the late summer. Your student union may also sell stationery at discount prices.

For some types of course (eg medicine, optometry and many science and technology courses) you may be expected to provide rather more in the way of equipment, which can involve you in considerable expense. Wait until you start the course before committing yourself to actually buying anything. Find out what's crucial to own and if possible, club together with other students to buy a piece of equipment. Your college or department should have some sort of deal with a manufacturer which allows students to purchase equipment at a substantial discount.

Do you need your own computer or word processor?

More and more university departments are insisting that work is presented typed rather than handwritten. Hardly surprising, when you consider how difficult it must be having to wade through thirty essays ranging anything from 2,000 to 10,000 words in varying degrees of legibility.

In addition, certain types of coursework (reports, projects, results of experiments etc) must be presented in a formal, predetermined fashion; not to do so could seriously affect your marks, regardless of the effort and originality of the work.

Accordingly, most colleges have computer facilities for students to make use of, often with 24 hour availability. This is all very well, but it does mean that a student could find him/herself having to book time for some ungodly hour to complete a piece of work. This has other unsatisfactory implications, not least your personal safety as you make your way home in the early hours.

Find out from your college exactly how you are expected to present your work. if they request it typed (they may request hard copy *and* the disc) seriously consider investing in your own computer or word processor. The expense may be unwelcome (check with your college in case it has a discount deal with a manufacturer), but once you've experienced the sheer convenience of having your own machine, not to mention the considerable time and drudgery a computer or word processor saves you, you'll never for one minute regret buying one.

LECTURES

The lecture forms the focus of your studies, and is the medium used to present a particular topic or theme and the current thinking on it – your lecturer's and other academics in the field. It's also your starting point for a more in-depth exploration of the subject through reading and discussions in tutorials and seminars. The lecturer will give you the relevant references to enable you to pursue your own researches.

A lecture normally lasts about an hour, during which you're expected to listen and take notes. There may be an opportunity at the end for questions, otherwise you'll get a chance to raise any points for clarification or discussion in tutorials. You may be asked to prepare for the next lecture by doing some specific reading. It's important that you do this because the lecturer will proceed on the assumption that you have the relevant background knowledge – if you haven't you'll be left wondering what on earth he/she is talking about.

Be prepared to get to lectures early – if only to make sure you get a seat. Lack of proper seating has become a real problem for many colleges in recent years as they have expanded student numbers without expanding facilities.

A word about lecturers

There are good lecturers and there are bad lecturers, and in between there are quite a few ranging from so-so to mediocre. Once in a while, if you're lucky, you'll get a brilliant lecturer, someone who captures your imagination and positively makes your brain tingle, someone who makes the most complex concept seem so simple that even an idiot can comprehend the sheer elegance of it.

Unfortunately university lecturers tend to be employed for their academic reputations, rather than their ability to teach. And, sorry to say, there are even those who regard time spent teaching as time away from their research project. A cynical comment maybe, but with all your preconceptions about higher education it can be disappointing to discover you're not being taught by some latterday Einstein.

However, your role as a student isn't just to sit there and be talked at – ineffectively or otherwise. Education at degree level is very much a two-way process, with *you* contributing, researching, questioning and formulating your own attitudes and opinions. If there are aspects of the lecture you don't understand (and you're not likely to be the only one), do feel you can ask the lecturer to explain or go through it again. You can do this at the relevant point in the lecture, or if you prefer, during the question period at the end or during your next tutorial. Either way, be happy that you are clear in your own mind about a particular theory, sequence of events or whatever. If you're not, this could jeopardise your understanding of fundamental aspects of the subject.

SEMINARS AND TUTORIALS

Seminars and tutorials are discussion groups where you talk over in some depth a specific topic you've all prepared for. You may have been asked to read extensively around a topic, research a particular scientific or engineering problem which you then solve as a group, or write an essay, which you are asked to present to the class for discussion.

Whereas lectures, as a rule, provide basic information on a topic, these smaller, more personal groups draw you into it, encouraging you to express your own ideas and interpretations. In other words, you're taught to think for yourself, and to develop interpersonal and communication skills which will be invaluable when you're earning a living. It's also the time you can bring up anything you're not clear about, either from a previous lecture or your personal reading.

If at first you feel shy about expressing yourself, bear in mind that other people are probably feeling the same. A classic ploy (which will stand you in good stead in meetings later in life) is to say something – anything – within the first three or four minutes. It breaks your personal ice, and you'll find it easier to say something more relevant next time. Most people tend to find that the longer they go without making that initial contribution to a discussion, the more difficult it becomes to open their mouths at all.

This probably sounds intimidating, but you'd be surprised how quickly you get into it, especially as you get to know each other as group. Boost your confidence by preparing thoroughly and rehearsing beforehand particular points you want to raise. And always remember that if you're challenged or criticised, it's nothing at all personal.

If you disagree with a point someone is making either in conversation or in an essay they're reading out, you are free to voice your opinion, but be constructive – and be prepared to back your comment with reasoned argument. You're not there to score points, so never be personal or over-the-top in your comments – not least because you might get the same treatment when it's your turn to present something you've laboured hard and long over.

USING THE LIBRARY

Pro rata, you will spend more time in your college library than anywhere else during your time at college – other, perhaps, than the student union bar. It will the calm centre in your otherwise frantic universe, the one place you can guarantee you won't get interrupted when you're studying, where you won't hear the thumping strains of someone else's stereo system, and where it will be warm enough that you don't have to wear woollen mittens. And because the only thing you can do there is work, you'll find it much easier to focus on your studies, motivated by all the people around you engrossed in doing the same.

Registering with the library will be a top priority in your first couple of days of Freshers Week. You'll then be entitled to use the library's facilities and take books out on loan. Most college libraries run a special introductory tour for new students, to explain the various procedures and the facilities on offer. If yours does, it's well worth taking advantage of (trying to work out the system by yourself wastes a lot of valuable time).

The facilities your library has to offer

Apart from providing an ideal working environment, the library will be your prime source of information. It holds not only hundreds of thousands of books, but periodicals, pamphlets, monographs, newspapers, government publications, cassettes, films and videos. A computerised catalogue (OPAC) will help you track down material quickly and efficiently. You'll also find that librarians are extremely helpful and generally have specialist knowledge of a wide range of academic subjects.

For courses that are especially popular there will be multiple copies of key books. The library will also have a restricted loans section for books which are in great demand or too rare or valuable to let off the premises. Naturally your library won't have absolutely everything, but it is certain to have access to the national inter-library loan service, via which it can obtain books from other libraries.

USEFUL STUDY TECHNIQUES

A surprising number of students complain that they start their university careers at major disadvantage: they've never been taught *how* to study. This is a real handicap at degree level, when you are expected to be able to assemble and absorb vast amounts of complex information. However, some universities run special courses on study techniques at the beginning of the new academic year to help students learn or brush up on basic study skills. Meanwhile, here are some useful guidelines.

Taking lecture notes

Don't even try to write down everything the lecturer says. Be selective, noting down key points (you can expand on them more fully later). Leave space so that you can add information (write on alternate lines, leave two or three lines between paragraphs). If the lecturer writes anything on the blackboard you can be certain this is important information which you should also be making a note of. Likewise, note down all reading references you're given (the title of the book or

publication, the date or issue number if relevant, the author's name, the recommended chapter), formulae, dates, names, theories and so on.

Your lecture notes will provide the core of your revision, so it's vital that they are clear, comprehensive and kept up to date. (If you miss a lecture for any reason, borrow the notes of a reliable friend.) It's a good idea to write up your notes more fulsomely as soon as possible after the lecture, while everything is still fresh in your mind (if you wait until you've got a stockpile of untranscribed notes you'll never get round to it).

Get into the habit of reviewing your course notes on a regular basis. This keeps the material fresh in your mind and makes revision a whole lot easier. Revision is also made considerably more manageable if your notes are well organised. Ringbinder files are very practical because you can build up your course material as you go along, inserting additional notes or photocopies of relevant readings.

Don't waste your time doing too much reading

Vast amounts of your personal study time will be taken up reading books, papers, periodicals etc. However, you'll soon realise you can't possibly read everything. You have to learn to be selective, to quickly get to the nub of a topic and not bother with any aspects which are irrelevant to your immediate needs. Before you start making notes, read the chapter or article through to get a basic idea of what it's about. Otherwise you'll end up writing far too much and waste valuable time. Equally, copying out great chunks of text is a time-waster. Put things into your own words, keeping your notes brief and to the point.

Always make an accurate note of the book's title, author and the relevant chapter and page numbers, as you may need to refer to it again. If you refer to a specific piece of information directly in an essay or dissertation, always acknowledge your source, either at an appropriate point in the text or as a footnote. Don't even try to pass off someone else's words or ideas as your own; your tutor is certain to recognise the true source. Sometimes, though, it is possible to incorporate accidently someone else's words into your own work. To prevent the likelihood of this happening, always put quotation marks either end of any passage you copy to distinguish it from your own writing.

Speed reading

Learning to speed read is an invaluable technique which will help you skim over irrelevant information until you reach what you're looking for. Most books are presented in a standard way to enable you to get quickly to the particular aspect of a subject.

- ❏ For a general introduction to a subject look at the *contents page*, which gives chapter headings, and sometimes sub-headings within each chapter.

- ❏ For specific references look up the *index* at the end of a book. Expect references to a specific theme to be scattered through-out the book (you'll have to check each individual one).

If the page numbers are printed in **bold type**, this indicates the author has discussed that particular theme (or an aspect of it) in some depth.

- ❐ In some books each chapter begins with an outline of major themes, so you know what it's going to cover. *Cross-headings* throughout the chapter provide further clues, pin-pointing information more specifically.

- ❐ If there are long and unbroken segments of text you can still use the skimming technique to save you having to read the whole lot. *The first and last sentences of paragraphs* give you a clue as to the main discussion point of the paragraph, and how the next one is going to develop.

Writing essays and dissertations

Essays and dissertations form an extremely important part of your coursework, and often contribute towards your final grades. Yet it's surprising how rarely students are taught how to communicate ideas in written form. It's assumed, rightly or wrongly, that by the time you reach university level you already know, and if you don't, no one may have the time or the inclination to put you wise.

- ❐ Don't make the mistake of thinking that brilliance will shine through a sloppy, disorganised prose style. It doesn't matter how original or creative you are, if you can't marshal your ideas in logical order, support them with appropriate facts and present your material in an accessible format, your ideas will have little impact on a lecturer who's having to wade through numerous similar efforts.

- ❐ Learn to develop a writing style that's easily readable, concise and straight to the point. You don't have to be ponderous to be taken seriously (not that you'd know it from the turgid style of some academic writers), but avoid using clichés and too many adjectives. Do make sure that you spell and use grammar correctly. University lecturers get fed up with what they regard as an unacceptable level of student illiteracy, and they're liable to mark accordingly.

- ❐ Before writing your first essay check whether your department expects it to be presented in a specific way (handwritten or typed, on a disc, lines single or double spaced etc).

You may be marked down for presenting your work inappropriately – even if no one's actually thought to brief you beforehand. If you handwrite it, make sure your writing is clear and easily legible.

❏ Bear in mind that you will probably have to do quite a bit of research before you sit down to write. Don't leave it until the last minute before you tackle an essay – the reference material may not be available, or you may not be able to get access to a college computer for the time you want it. You should also reckon on a piece of work taking roughly twice as long as you anticipated, so allot adequate amount of time in your work schedule.

❏ When you start writing, working out a framework of the main points you intend to cover helps focus your thoughts. Remember you also have to have an introduction (always difficult to write – you might find it easier to come back to it when you've finished writing the rest) and a final paragraph or two which briefly summarises the major points and draws them to an appropriate conclusion.

❏ You may not be able to complete an essay in one sitting, but try and put aside a decent chunk of time when you can work on it without interruption. Once you get into the rhythm, your thoughts tend to flow and the essay progresses surprisingly quickly. (It will take much longer if you do it piecemeal.) If you do get stuck or find you're noticeably slowing down, take a break or get on with something else. It's sensible to know when to call a halt; struggling on can be counter productive, and the quality of your work isn't usually so good.

REVISION AND EXAMS

If you have managed to organise your studies into a comfortable and steady routine, attended lectures and tutorials, handed in essays and other coursework on time, done all the necessary reading and kept your lecture notes up to scratch and reviewed them regularly, you should be able to take revision in your stride. In fact this is really where establishing a study routine starts paying off, for you should by now be confident and knowledgeable about your various course topics. Not for you the traditional pre-exam panic of trying to catch up on crucial readings you somehow missed out on, trying to make sense of concepts you didn't grasp at the time and didn't get round to asking your course tutor about.

Some people sail through exams, others never seem to do themselves justice. You've had enough experience over the years to know which category you fall in. If it's the latter, there's a good chance that your shortcomings in exams are balanced by the coursework you've completed during the term, and which also counts towards your final grades. But there's still a great deal you can do yourself to improve your grades – that doesn't involve slogging away even harder.

An exam is not dissimilar to a crossword puzzle. The world is similarly divided into people who can can toss off The Times crossword in the time it takes to microwave a pizza, and those for whom their local free sheet's crossword will forever be one of life's great intellectual mysteries. The truth of the matter is that it's simply a matter of technique, of getting into the mind of the crossword compiler and understand what *he's* getting at, rather than what *you* think he should be getting at. Crack the code, read the clues and suddenly it all becomes clear.

The mistake many people make when answering questions on an exam paper is that they fail to understand what the examiner wants, and proceed to interpret and answer the question in their own way. This could be a simple matter of not having revised the topic thoroughly enough, so you're left in effect answering the question as best you can (nearly always a waste of time – you might as well not have bothered). But all too often, as any professional examiner will tell you, it's a matter of not having taken enough time to read the question properly, and failing to spot clues which provide you with your line of approach.

If you think this is the reason your exam results never seem to reflect the amount of hard work you put into revision, get hold of past exam papers and practise analysing and answering the questions. Your personal or course tutor will be able to help you. If your department doesn't use old exam papers as part of the revision process and you're aware that you're not alone in having a problem with your exam technique, why not get together and ask a lecturer to give you a special tutorial.

Planning your revision

☐ Work out a revision timetable well in advance of your exams. With proper planning, you'll stay on top of your revision programme and you won't find yourself having to burn the midnight oil.

☐ Your lecture notes will be the basis for all your revision; give them a quick review to see if there are any gaps, weaknesses or aspects you realise you don't quite understand, and do the necessary work to plug them.

☐ Unless you're some kind of genius, you'll be putting in longer hours during the pre-exam period. This is fine, but you'll work more effectively if you build regular periods into your timetable when you can relax, have fun and generally give your brain a break.

☐ Try to work in regular short bursts of about one to two hours. Your powers of concentration fall off significantly after this, and you won't absorb information so effectively. Get up and have a walk about, make yourself a snack or a coffee.

☐ As you revise each course, make abbreviated notes which you can use as a memory aid on the eve of the exam. Fill a few filing cards or two sides of a piece of A4 paper with key facts and formulae, dates, names, theories etc.

Coping with stress

There's no getting away from the fact that revision and exams are a time of great stress – however much you've got your studies under control. But you need a certain amount of stress to motivate yourself. The thing is to achieve the right balance. Too much stress and your brain feels as though it's a quagmire, struggling to absorb and retain important facts. Too much stress and you spread yourself too widely instead of focusing on the task or topic in hand. Too much stress and you start to feel the strain physically, experiencing sleepless nights and generally feeling lethargic and permanently tired.

If you make a point of looking after yourself physically, your brain can concentrate on studying. That means getting a regular good night's sleep and getting plenty of rest and relaxation – even if it's just pottering around your flat, watching something undemanding on television or sitting in the sun for an hour. You should also aim for some regular exercise. Exercise, whether it's swimming, running, playing tennis or dancing, is a great way of relieving all the tension and frustration that build up inside you after long hours of sitting in one position, deep in concentration. Your mind benefits enormously too – both from the contrast and from being forced to think about something else for a while.

It's important to eat regularly and healthily too. If you don't have time for cooking, make sure you have a supply of reasonably nutritious fast foods; fruit, nuts, bread, peanut butter, jams, tinned soups, baked beans, pizzas, biscuits — ready-prepared chilled meals if your budget allows (consider the cost balanced by the time saved and the reassurance that at least you've had something to eat). If you're living in a hall of residence which has a canteen, you'll be sure of getting at least one good meal a day. If you're self-catering, arrange to do some of your revision on campus, so that you can have a hot meal at the college canteen.

It's tempting to drink gallons of tea or coffee to keep your mind alert, but the stimulants in them can make you edgy and add to the stress factor. Try their de-caffinated equivalents, or switch to mineral water, fruit juices or milk. Avoid alcohol during the day; it depresses the nervous system, affecting your concentration – the last thing you need when you're revising and under pressure. If you want to have a drink, save it for the evening, after you've finished work for the day, so you can relax and enjoy it. Don't go on a binge, however much you may feel you've earned it – especially the night before an exam. There's nothing worse, next morning, than feeling groggy when you should be feeling mentally alert and raring to go.

What can you do if you really get into a panic?

University authorities are well aware of the pressures on students at exam time. So if things really start getting on top of you and you have problems coping, don't keep it to yourself.

Your personal tutor will be sympathetic, and should be able to reassure you that work-wise, you've got little to worry about, especially if you've worked consistently throughout the term or year.

Alternatively you can talk things through with your college or student union welfare officer. Some college health centres run a special counselling service at exam times, during which you can be helped to put things in perspective and learn relaxation techniques.

If you get an attack of anxiety the night before an exam, panicking because you can't remember anything at all – *stop what you're doing*. It's your brain's way of saying it's suffering from overload. Don't even attempt to struggle on; you'll take in less and less and feel worse than ever. The first thing to bear in mind is that you can't possibly have forgotten everything, especially if you've been revising according to plan. You've got a momentary mental block, that's all.

Put your books away and take a break. Have a long bath, watch some TV, cook yourself a simple supper (cooking can be very therapeutic), have an early night with a book or magazine (nothing academic). Set your alarm for a little earlier the next morning, and briefly review your notes for the impending exam. After a good night's sleep your mind will have freed up considerably, and you won't have any trouble remembering crucial facts.

EXAM STRATEGY

The night before the exam (or in the morning, if you prefer) read through your abbreviated exam notes one last time to refresh your memory. Before you leave for the exam hall, make sure you have all the necessary equipment (writing tools, calculator, a packet of paper handkerchiefs, a packet of sweets etc). Allow yourself plenty of time to get to college. If, when you arrive there, everyone else is fraught and anxious, take yourself off to one side so you aren't infected by their panic.

❑ When you're given the go-ahead to turn over the exam paper, take a deep breath and read it through very carefully. Go through it twice, taking as much time as you need. Read the instructions very carefully, noting which questions are compulsory etc. Start provisionally marking ones you think you can answer.

❑ If the worse happens, and you don't see any at all, try not to panic. Take another deep breath and relax for a moment. Then slowly read through the paper again. As you read it there are bound to be areas you start to recognise and can write something about. Take things slowly and calmly and you'll realise you can build up quite adequate answers.

❑ When you've decided which questions to answer, work out the time allocation for each one. If you overrun, leave it and go on to the next question (return to the unfinished one at the end if there's time). It's vitally important to answer *all* the questions you're asked to, even if you can't answer one or two completely (you tend to pick up most marks in the first half). Don't concentrate on answering two questions fulsomely and brilliantly, in the hope that achieving maximum marks (if you're so lucky) will make up for your other answers being mediocre – or even non-existent. Unfortunately marking doesn't work that way.

❑ Before starting to answer each question, make a brief plan, outlining the points you intend to cover (then put a neat line through it when you've finished writing the answer).

❑ When the exam is over try not to get involved in a post mortem with other students. However you think you've done, it's over, so put it behind you and go home and relax and have something to eat. Then you get on with preparing for the next exam.

When your exams are finally over and done with, organise a celebration with your course, flat or hall mates. You've earned it!

Chapter 8

CHANGING COURSES

Is your course really the problem? – finding out what went wrong – switching to another course – transferring to another university – changing your mind before term begins – waiting until you're ready for college – how changing course or college affects your grant

Making the right decision isn't always easy, especially when you're under pressure. Making decisions that can have long-term consequences on your career are all the more difficult when what's really concerning you is getting halfway decent A Level grades. So sometimes you end up making the wrong decision.

Around 20% of first year students have second thoughts about their course, sometimes even their choice of university. The problem is, do you make the best of it and spend the next three years studying a course that leaves you feeling at best indifferent, and at worst, bored, dissatisfied and miserable? Or should you risk disappointing your parents and your school by dropping out during your first or second term, and taking a break from the education system until you have a better idea of what you want to do?

Let's get one thing straight. Admitting you've made a mistake isn't a weakness – it takes guts. And if it's any help, none of the students interviewed during the research for this book who had changed their course or college had experienced any regrets afterwards about their decision. In fact, they were invariably much happier. University authorities, for their part, aren't in the business of forcing unwilling students to – literally – stay the course. There are recognised procedures in place for helping students who want to change courses within a university, or who want to change university altogether.

If your instinct is telling you that you've chosen the wrong course or university, don't ignore it. But before you make any firm decision, talk things through with as many people as you can, just in case your problem turns out to be something quite different – and less drastic in the solution.

IS YOUR COURSE REALLY THE PROBLEM?

You may have convinced yourself you've chosen the wrong course, but have you really given it (and you) a chance?

In the first few weeks of college you're swamped by new experiences, and sometimes it can all seem a bit too much. Add to this the fact that you're probably missing your family and friends and the comforts of home. What you could be feeling is a big lack of confidence, which isn't made any better when you're trying to get the hang of a new subject and a very different, more intense teaching and studying style than you were used to at A Level.

It helps no end to talk to someone sympathetic and who understands the problems you're facing. Your personal tutor is just the person, but you can also speak to the college's welfare officer or student counsellor, the student union's welfare or education officer or even the college chaplain. Simply by having an opportunity to air your worries, you may find that the root of your problem is that you are expecting too much of yourself too quickly.

If this doesn't help, maybe the problem is something else that's solvable, perhaps to do with the actual way you study. If you're having trouble grasping a crucial concept, for instance, this is going to have a knock-on effect on your ability to understand the rest of the course. It could be that you need to learn to ask questions, either during the lecture or the next tutorial. (After all, you may not be the only student in the dark.) Your lecturer may even be prepared to help you out with a private tutorial.

Before you finally throw in the towel, make one last effort and find out exactly what topics your course covers right through to your third year. It's amazing how little information some colleges give their students about the course contents. Many degree courses are quite varied, and there are frequently opportunities to select other course options, sometimes outside your own department or faculty. In effect, you're shaping your own degree. Often courses tend to be mandatory in the first year, but you may feel it's worth gritting your teeth through a course topic you don't particularly like, or find difficult, to get to the topics that really interest to you a little further on in the course.

WHAT WENT WRONG?

Before giving up your course it's important to try and understand why it hasn't worked out, so that you don't make the same mistake twice. Here are some possible reasons:

❏ You didn't give that much thought to what you really wanted to study. You may have chosen your course because it was your best or favourite A Level subject, and now you realise your interest isn't enough to sustain another three years of exclusive, in-depth study.

❏ You may have gone along with the school's careers teacher's (or your parents') suggestion because you didn't have an alternative one or you were too busy coping with your A Levels.

❏ Having deferred your course and taken a year off to work or travel, you now find your priorities and interests have changed and the course is no longer relevant.

❏ The subject is being taught at a level way beyond your ability to absorb and make sense of the information, and as a consequence you've got increasingly behind with the work.

HOW EASY IS IT TO TRANSFER TO ANOTHER COURSE?

Theoretically not too difficult, although in practice some departments make it more so than it need be. Once you've made your decision you have to act quickly if you want to be able to transfer straight away. If you leave it too long you won't have a hope of catching up with the work that's already been covered on your new course. You'll have to start college all over again the following autumn, with virtually a whole year lost in between. Keep on at the relevant authorities, so they know how important it is for you to change *now*. If you need advice, or help in speeding things up, the university's careers office should be able to help, also the welfare officer or the student union welfare or education officer.

The procedure

The first step is to inform your personal tutor and department head of your decision. Then you can contact the department head of the course you want to transfer to. There are three conditions you have to fulfil. (1) You have to have the appropriate academic qualifications. (2) There has to be a space available on the course. (3) The department running the course has to want you, and be satisfied that you are suitably motivated to make the change. A word of warning. It's often thought that the best way of getting on to a popular, oversubscribed course is to apply for an 'easier' course and transfer as soon as you get to college. Wrong. If it's full, it's full; you'll probably be advised to leave college and apply all over again next year. And if your qualifications weren't impressive enough to get you on the course by applying directly the first time, you'll have to use the year off to (a) improve your grades or (b) do something eyecatching and enterprising to increase your desirability.

CHANGING TO ANOTHER UNIVERSITY

Sometimes it isn't the course that's the problem, it's the place. If you're used to the slower pace of a country town or village you may find the relative frenzy of a big city like London a bit too stimulating, and vice versa. Or perhaps you find life too claustrophobic at a traditional campus-style university, and would be happier in a less structured environment. Where you study is just as important as what you study – you're going to have to spend the next three or so years there.

Theoretically it is just about possible to transfer to a new university if you act within the first couple of weeks of the first term if the initial course structures and contents are very similar. If they are not, you will have to leave your current college and fill in the time until you can start again next year.

If you know which course and college you want to apply to, contact the course admissions tutor direct. He or she will tell you what you need to do to get a place, and whether there's one available. It could be a relatively straightforward procedure; given you already have your A Levels and you've been accepted once for a university place so you've already demonstrated the requisite level of academic ability. You will have to satisfy the qualification requirements for the course, and have the written endorsement of your current course tutor or department head.

If you want to spend some time thinking about what to do and where to go next, you will have to leave your current place (you could lose your eligibility for a full-term grant if you leave it too late – see the section on grants) and re-apply next year.

YOU CAN DO THE RIGHT THINGS – AND STILL GET IT WRONG!

However carefully you think about what you want to study, sometimes you can still end up making the wrong decision.

Ross Matthews had certainly done all the right things. Not sure what he wanted to do, and keen to have a break from studying after his A Levels, he took a year off to make up his mind, and to earn some money and travel. Eventually he decided on a degree course in Business Studies, and got a place at a college of higher education.

> "During the first few weeks I realised I had made a big mistake. The work was hard, and I quickly started falling behind. I spoke to my tutor, and he told me there was no point in staying on the course. He actually recommended me to change to something more appropriate, although he warned me I may have left it a little late. I decided I wanted to study English instead, but the English department told me that the course was full and I'd have to apply again next year.
>
> "I wasn't too happy about this, as I'd already taken one year out. I kept on pushing, though; it took me a whole week to arrange a meeting with the head of English, and by this time I was getting so fed up I was considering leaving the college anyway. After a week of constant nagging, the English department eventually let me on to the course. I'm glad I persisted – I'm really enjoying the course and I've now settled in."

Ross's advice is that if you want to change your course, do it within the first three weeks if possible: "There's more chance of a place being available, and less chance of falling behind. Try to get to know people quickly on the new course so you can borrow their lecture notes to catch up."

And while his lecturers were quick to advise him not to carry on with a course that was clearly wrong for him, Ross feels more effort could have been put in to getting him switched to a more appropriate course. "There seemed to be little concern about me wasting another year, stuck between courses. It's really important, therefore, to persevere so you can get on a course straightaway. You must make sure the university authorities realise just how important changing courses is to you."

CHANGING YOUR MIND BEFORE YOU START COLLEGE

Sometimes the whole rigmarole of revision, exams and university applications can just take you over, and it's only when you finally have a chance to relax and take stock that you find yourself having second thoughts about that much-coveted place at university. Do you really want to go? Can you face another three years on the academic treadmill? What on earth are your family and teachers going to say if you decide not to go after all?

You're bound to feel stale, thoroughly sick, even, of education, and who can blame you? Sometimes this passes, and after a few weeks' break you find you are getting excited again at the propect of going to university. But if your enthusiasm hasn't been rekindled, and to make matters worse, you're having doubts about the actual course, what should you do?

The first thing to do is not to rush into something you've got such strong reservations about. And second, to resist any pressure, albeit well-meaning, from your parents and teachers to continue with your original plan. True, your interest might perk up once you're at college, but you're more likely to become even more disillusioned and possibly drop out altogether.

Instead, consider taking the pressure off yourself by deferring your place at university for a year (but let the authorities know as soon as possible so it can be re-allocated). This will give you the chance to (a) find out how you really feel about your subject and (b) see if there isn't something else you'd rather study, and somewhere else you'd rather study it.

Rachael Anderson found herself in exactly this disillusioned state after finishing her A Levels. "I was due to go to Leeds University to study History and Politics, which I did at A Level. I still think I'd have quite enjoyed doing them. Then I realised I had no enthusiasm to go to college whatsoever. I don't think I've have enjoyed it if I'd gone then. The whole idea of students was just awful.

"It took a year of working at a job that was pretty crap to realise that perhaps I did want to go after all! I went abroad for a year, which was great, but I wasted the year after that working. But I think I needed to waste that year to realise I wanted to go to college. I chose Tourism, Business and Management (at Oxford Brookes University) because I thought it would be useful, and I wanted to do something more vocational than History and Politics. Deciding not to go straight on to university after school was the best thing I could have done."

Waiting until you're good and ready

There are no regulations that say you have to go to university within a set period of time. In fact there are lots of advantages going to college as a mature student. You're more likely to know what you want to do and, perhaps more important, why you want to do it. You'll be better motivated as far as studying is concerned, which will compensate for the time you've spent away from textbooks. You won't be fazed by the newness, challenges and irritations of college life. Universities will positively welcome the contribution that your experience and worldliness can make to college life in general and lectures and tutorials in particular (to the extent of making application procedures more flexible). And you can get a bigger grant if you're 26-plus and have worked for three years!

HOW IS YOUR GRANT AFFECTED IF YOU CHANGE YOUR COURSE?

It shouldn't be at all, provided you get the written permission of your department, the permission of your LEA *and* you act within certain time limits. However, the rules are somewhat complex concerning these time limits, so it's important that you contact your LEA as soon as possible to find out what their own particular limits are.

LEAs accept that you can make a mistake in your choice of course or college, and that you shouldn't be penalised by having your grant proportionately reduced by the time you've already spent at college. Therefore provided you leave your first course by no later than the the seventh week of the second term, you can have a brand new, full length grant for your new course.

However, Department of Education guidelines do actually allow for a student switching course and college as late as 16 months from the start of the original course and still receiving a full length grant, provided certain conditions are satisfied – and the LEA, who has to pick up the bill, agrees.

Repaying your grant

If you have decided to give up studying for a degree for the time being, or you are leaving college temporarily, to start a new course the following autumn, you will have to repay the portion of your grant which remains unused – the amount allocated for the rest of the term and the ensuing holiday. (If you've already spent the money, you will still have to find it somehow.) You should contact your LEA immediately, who will tell you how much this is. The university registrar is also required to inform the LEA of your change in circumstances, so one way or another, the latter will know it has some money due!

A major portion of your grant is likely to have been accounted for by your hall of residence fees. However, you should be able to get a refund, provided the hall can re-let your room right away (not usually a problem at most universities).

Chapter 9
TAKING A YEAR OFF

Why it could be a good idea – can you handle taking a year out? – the importance of planning – the attitude of universities – persuading your parents – getting a job – voluntary work – travelling and working abroad – travel facts

There's no law that says you have to go straight to university after you've finished your A Levels. Around 25% of independent school students and 10% of state school students take a year off to do voluntary work, travel and/or earn some money, before taking up their studies again. You don't put at risk your chances of obtaining a place at university – or a grant – because you decide to opt out for a while.

In fact, there are extremely valid reasons for taking a break from full-time education. If you have any reservations at all about going straight to university in the autumn, don't go just for the sake of it, or to keep your parents and teachers happy. Be prepared, though, to give good reasons why it wouldn't be right for you just now. If you think you'll have difficulty explaining in a convincing, reasonable manner, the following common experiences may help you sort out and put into words your own feelings.

You may feel you've had just about all the education you can stand

After more than thirteen years in the education system, crowned by the intensity of studying, revising and sitting exams for your A Levels, don't be surprised if you find yourself balking at the prospect of going straight into another three years of high pressure learning.

Usually the long summer break is enough to get you thinking positively again, and looking forward to going to university in the autumn. In any event, it's going to be a very different way of studying and living from what you've experienced before, and nothing at all like the school treadmill you've just said goodbye to.

If, though, your attitude is as jaded as ever, you could benefit from a sabbatical from education to restore your motivation. Struggling with a course that fails to ignite your interest and enthusiasm could end up with you dropping out of college and being put off higher education for life.

More and more people are choosing to take a breathing space from education for a year – or even longer. Universities, for their part, are happy with this (so long as the time is spent 'interestingly'), because they end up with maturer students who can cope with independence and are generally more motivated in their studying.

You may be having second thoughts about your choice of course

Working for A Levels is demanding enough, without having to make serious decisions about what subject you want to study at university. If you're vocationally inclined (you want to be a doctor, an engineer or a social worker) your decision is more or less made for you. If you don't have strong feelings, career-wise, the choice is wide open. It's all the more important that you spend as much time as you need sifting the options. And time is something you don't have much of when you're studying hard *and* trying to get your applications in by the deadline.

It's easy to feel you've got on to an education conveyor belt. That other people (parents, teachers) are making crucial assumptions, decisions even, on your behalf. Somewhere along the way you've lost control of your life. Has anybody actually asked *you* what you *really* want to do? If you've experienced the type of cursory careers interview at your school or sixth form college that many students complain of, you may have found it impossible to admit that you don't actually know what subject you want to study at university. Mainly because you don't yet have any firm idea of what you want to do with your life. It's easier, in a way, to let someone else make the decision for you, especially when you've got more pressing things like exams to think about – or you haven't an alternative to suggest.

If any of this strikes a chord of recognition, you need to buy yourself some time. The long summer vacation may be as much time as you need to rethink what you would really like to study at college, and if necessary, to research new courses and new universities/colleges which you can then apply for through Clearing in late summer.

If you're still undecided, then seriously consider taking a year off to travel, get a job, experience a bit of real life. Anything but start a degree course under duress, only to drop out disillusioned a few months later. That can have a damaging and long-lasting effect on your self confidence. There's nothing to stop you applying again next year – or in ten years time, if that's how long it takes you to make the commitment to a degree.

Your grades aren't good enough or you don't get a place through Clearing

If you've received a conditional offer and your A level grades don't match the college's requirements you have a chance of getting a place somewhere else through Clearing, especially if you are prepared to be flexible about the course and the college.

NICHOLAS JONES
'A' LEVEL RESULTS

ENGLISH	Z
HISTORY	Z
FRENCH	Z

Alternatively you could consider retaking your A Levels (or the particular subjects that didn't come up to expectation) and then reapply next year with your new, improved grades. Retaking exams wouldn't mean having to go into school everyday, as you used to. It's more a matter of working on your weaker areas through personal study, practising your exam and essay technique and perhaps having a regular one-to-one class with the relevant teacher.

Depending on the time your examination board schedules for A Level retakes (usually November or January), you still have nine months or more to spend on sabbatical. And you may even have time to fit in a part-time job while you're studying (so long as it doesn't jeopardise your studies).

If you don't do it now...

This is the one – and possibly the only – time in your life when you can opt out of the mainstream of life for a while without worrying about the consequences. Right now you have no family responsibilities, no mortgage or cosy lifestyle to pay for and no career to worry about.

It's true that some people take their year off after they've graduated, as a final fling before getting into the nine-to-five routine. But with graduate unemployment being what it is and unlikely to improve over the next few years, when you do eventually graduate you could find you decide not to waste time getting on to the job-seeking bandwagon – missing out on your one chance to escape the system for a while.

CAN YOU HANDLE TAKING A YEAR OFF?

Taking a break from education can give you more than you bargained for. At the very least it will broaden your outlook, but the experience could also alter the course of your life, sending you in a direction you might otherwise never have considered. You will meet people and have experiences which could cause you to question your personal beliefs and attitudes. Any pre-ordained plans and ambitions could be irrevocably disrupted.

But then who's to say that's not for the better?

The disadvantages of taking time out

It's important to know in your own mind why you want a break from studying. The advantages are pretty obvious, but there are disadvantages too.

❐ Money can be a major problem. Unless you can depend on the largesse of your parents, you will have to support yourself during the entire period. If your plan is to find a job so that you can save some money to fund you through college you may find it difficult (a) getting any sort of job at all and (b) finding a job that does more than cover basic living expenses, so that you can actually save some money. You may have similar problems if you want to work for a while to get enough money together to go travelling.

❐ You will be a year behind school friends who have gone straight to university. How much of a problem this is depends on how close you are to your friends. But bear in mind that simply by being at different colleges most of you will quite naturally drift apart, especially as you all make new friends.

❐ If you do find a job that not only pays reasonably well but has some prospects, you may find the idea of being an impoverished student less than appealing. You may also be tempted, having got on the first rung of a career ladder of sorts, to opt out of further education and take your chance in the real world.

❐ Travelling to exciting, far-flung places could sidetrack you from your plans to start university next year. You might not want to come back at all, or worse still, university could seem restricting and a real anticlimax, and you could have problems settling down. For that reason it's a good idea to return to the UK a few weeks before college starts, so you have a chance to get yourself back down to earth and into the right frame of mind for studying. If that doesn't work, there's no reason why you shouldn't extend your break to two years, and get the wanderlust out of your system.

Persuading your parents

Not all parents are keen on the idea of a year off between school and university. Some are suspicious that it's merely an excuse to do not very much at all; others worry that their son or daughter might decide not to return to education at the end of it. It will help your cause if you can explain exactly why you want to take some time off, how you're planning to use it, and how what you accomplish during it will be a positive benefit when you do eventually go to college.

If you're planning to backpack and spend different amounts of time in different countries as the whim takes you, your parents are quite rightly going to be concerned about your safety, especially if your experience of travel has so far been restricted to package holidays. With political and social unrest on the increase even in previously stable countries, you could be risking more than having your travellers cheques stolen.

It will reassure them immensely (though they'll still worry) if you show that you've planned your trip in detail, researched the countries you're intending to visit, organised the necessary documentation and health requirements and so on. They'll be even more reassured if you're travelling with a friend, staying in properly run youth hostels – and if you arrange to telephone them on a regular basis to let them know everything is OK. Expect – and take with good grace – lectures and all manner of advice. And if you do find yourself in a country where there's some kind of unrest, always call your parents to say you're safe, even if the disturbance is hundreds of miles away at the opposite end of the country.

How will your university react?

Generally speaking, most universities regard a year out between school and college as a good idea. Moving from the relatively sheltered existence of home and school, and straight into the independence of college life can come as quite a shock to many students. By having a year or so's break in between, colleges recognise that a young person can learn to stand on his or her own two feet, experience something of the real world, and arrive at college a better student. However, all universities without exception will expect you to have done something useful, interesting and character-building during that time. If you simply fritter it away in an unorganised manner, staying in bed until noon and watching games shows all afternoon before meeting your mates in the pub, they will not be impressed. Look at it from their point of view. Such lack of focus and more especially imagination doesn't bode too well for the commitment and agility of mind it takes to study for a degree.

How late can you leave the decision to take a year off?

That depends on whether you've had a firm offer of a place. Universities are required to fill courses in order to receive government funding, so the last thing they want at the last minute is loads of empty places. Similarly, for every student toying with the idea of taking a year out, there are many more who'd give anything to be taking over that place. Their only chance of doing this is through the Clearing process – provided you've notified the university authorities in enough time to release your place.

A university will, in principle, defer a place for a year, provided you've given it decent notice *and* a good enough reason for doing so. Before you finally decide to take a year off, do speak to your admissions tutor first, to find out the college's policy on deferred places – and to make sure that your place will be held available for next year.

If, however, you haven't got a place anywhere and you want to take a year off, don't bother with going through Clearing (which is for filling current places). You can apply again fresh for next year, although bear in mind, if you plan to travel, that you may be required to attend interviews. This could mean working in the UK first, until you've got a place fixed up, and doing your travelling afterwards. Otherwise you would have to be prepared to return to the UK for interviews when the time comes.

THE IMPORTANCE OF PLANNING YOUR YEAR

As soon as you know you want to take a year off, start making plans. A year may seem like a long time, but it slips away remarkably fast if you delay getting your act together. Almost anything you might want to do – travel, voluntary work, earn some money – takes time to organise and there are often deadlines for applications. If you want to find a job, for example, you'll give yourself a vital headstart on all the other school leavers looking for work by contacting potential employers several months before your last exam.

A trip abroad requires meticulous planning. If you want to work your way around Europe, for example, you'll need to research the types of work likely to be available in the various countries, and at what time of the year. You can then plan your trip on a practical basis, maximising your chances of finding work – otherwise you'll quickly run out of money and have to return home before you had planned to.

If you intend travelling further afield you will need to know each individual country's visa requirements. Applications will have to processed via the embassy or consulate of each individual country you're hoping to visit and, depending on the country, this can be time-consuming. If you want to find a job, you'll have to check if there are any restrictions on your doing so. Keep abreast of any political, religious or social problems which could erupt in the near future, and be prepared to change your itinerary accordingly.

WORKING IN THE UK DURING YOUR YEAR OFF

Getting a job isn't easy, especially when you're competing with thousands of other school-leavers. It'll be even more difficult if you live in an area of high unemployment.

Your university-to-be will be expecting you to find a job that has some relevance to your course or intended career, or one where you can acquire valuable experience in dealing with colleagues and the general public.

Realistically, though, you may not be able to be that choosy – and anyway, you can pick up useful experience in almost any type of job. Should your college quibble about the kind of work you propose doing, you could point out that the money you earn will be the deciding factor as to whether or not you can afford to take up your place at university next year.

FRIED CHICKEN CAFÉ

Start planning early if you want to start working as soon as you leave school. Be realistic about what sort of job you're likely to get. You'll be bottom of the office/department/store hierarchy and will be expected to do the mundane and boring jobs that nobody else wants to do. Go out of your way to be enthusiastic and helpful (you're not going to be there for the rest of your working life) and you may find yourself being offered work during the university vacations.

Write a CV which gives your educational qualifications, personal interests and any work experience you've had so far. Include a couple of references from people who know you well (your head or form teacher and a part-time employer would be ideal); ask your referees for permission before including them in your CV. Your CV should be clearly laid out and typed, and two pages at the most. Express your work experience positively, even if you don't think it sounds so impressive. If you've had a Saturday job in WH Smiths, say, describe the various things you've done in such a way that a potential employer gets a feel for your wider abilities. Working on the till means you are confident with electronic systems and with working under pressure (mention the fact that Saturdays are usually busy); dealing with queries suggests you're helpful and know the importance of keeping the customer satisfied; making sure shelves are always stocked demonstrates initiative and an understanding of the importance of product presentation to your employer's business, and so on. Put this way – and without any unnecessary embellishments, your Saturday job shows you to be a responsible, willing and enterprising employee.

Research thoroughly local companies, department stores etc where there could be job possibilities. Go through your local newspapers' Situations Vacant' column and make a list of the companies that are advertising (the job specified may not be suitable but there could be other work available). Go through local business directories (your reference library will have some), and also the local Thomson telephone directory, which has a business section.

Draw up a shortlist of companies to target first. You're more likely to impress a potential employer if you can address a letter to someone by name. Newspaper advertisements may give you the name of the personnel director or managing director. Otherwise you could ask your parents if you could telephone and ask for the correct person to write to (depending how the conversation goes, you may be able to ask there and then about work prospects; if you discover there's nothing doing, you've saved one unnecessary letter).

The letter accompanying your CV should be brief (one page only), straight to the point and pleasant. Say (without being gushing) why you would like to work for that company, briefly outline experience which would be of practical use to them, and give the date you would be available to start work.

Should you tell them you are hoping to go to university next year? A bit difficult, this, because some companies might get sniffy if they think you're merely 'filling in time' at their expense. On the other hand, because of the recession there are companies who appreciate the chance to take on short-term staff. The best advice is to be honest; staff turnover at the relatively humble level you'll be working is usually quite high, so the year you're planning to offer them represents a fair commitment.

Make the most of contacts

You could strike lucky and land a job quickly using the method described above. However, it's a fact of life at all career levels that the best jobs are to be found through personal contacts, for which include friends of friends of friends. In other words it's *who* you know rather than what you know.

You probably think you don't know anyone influential, but that's not true. Compile a comprehensive list of aunts, uncles, cousins, older brothers and sisters, grandparents, neighbours and your friends' parents. Now find out what they do for a living. Somewhere on that list there will be people who will hear on their office grapevine of jobs that may be coming up in the near future. Most people would rather employ someone they know than an absolute stranger; even if they've never met you before, you come recommended by someone they know. So let everybody who could possibly be of any use to you know that you're on the look-out for work, and that you're prepared to be enthusiastic and flexible.

When you attend an interview

Most offices are run along very conservative lines, and you will be expected to fit in with the company's dress code. Be neat, clean and tidy (shave if appropriate), and wear reasonably formal clothes (a shirt, tie, jacket and trousers for men; a blouse, skirt and jacket for women).

Make sure you have the correct address, know how to get to the company and then allow yourself adequate time. When you meet your interviewer, smile and shake hands firmly, and sit down when you're invited to do so. You're bound to feel nervous, but listen carefully, take a deep breath when you speak and avoid answering questions monosyllabically. Be friendly and enthusiastic (but don't overdo it).

Companies like it if you show interest in them, over and above wanting a job, so have a couple of questions prepared. When the interview is over, shake hands again and thank the interviewer for his or her time. Write a brief thank-you letter – it helps fix you in the interviewer's mind.

VOLUNTARY WORK IN THE COMMUNITY

If you want a complete break from the education treadmill but you'd like to do something really worth while, you'll have no problems finding work in a wide range of voluntary projects in the community. In fact you'll be welcomed with open arms. You don't have to have any experience, just a commitment to work hard for an agreed period of time and be good-natured in all circumstances. What you get in return is the satisfaction of knowing that you've made a small contribution to society, and a real and often humbling insight into what life is like for people who don't have your advantages. You'll learn more about human nature, good and bad, yours included, that you ever would in three years in a lecture hall.

If you want to work close to home, perhaps combining voluntary work with a part-time paid job, contact your council's social services department. It's certain to have a volunteer bureau that's eager to hear from people with a regular amount of time to spare – if only a few hours a week. You should have no problem finding work that fits in with your interests and experience, particularly as more and more services are cut back. Volunteers are much needed in day centres (for the elderly and the mentally or physically disabled), hospitals (befriending and running errands for patients, running shops and trolleys, providing beauty care), for helping elderly or housebound people in the community (shopping, chatting, providing transport etc), in youth clubs (helping with activities and sports, running coffee bars), children's playgroups and to work on local conservation projects.

Working as a full-time volunteer

If you can commit yourself to full-time voluntary work for a period of four to 12 months, and you don't mind working away from home, the national volunteer agency Community Service Volunteers (CSV) has 700 projects throughout the UK. All volunteers are accepted (2,500 are recruited each year), and in return for their services receive board, accommodation and travel expenses, plus weekly pocket money.

You'll be interviewed so that your interests, skills and experiences can be matched to where they are needed most, and can be working within a month. CSV volunteers work alongside professional staff, helping people in need in homes, hostels, night shelters, hospital and day centres. Depending on your placement you may be working with young offenders, children with special educational needs, people leaving longstay hospitals, the elderly or the disabled. To find out more write to CSV Head Office, 237 Pentonville Road, London N1 9NJ (telephone 071-278 6601).

TRAVELLING AND WORKING ABROAD

Spend some time thinking *how* you want to travel, especially if to date your experience has been of the package holiday kind. Do you want to spend a period of time travelling through a particular group of countries, stopping for a while and then moving on as your fancy takes you? Do you want to travel alone, or in the company of a friend? Rather than move from place to place, would you prefer to work in a particular country, and in the process get to know something of its people and culture?

Do you want to make your own arrangements, or would you be happier going through an organisation that specialises in placing young people on projects abroad?

Whatever you decide to do, you can't just get up and go. To get the most out of your travels – and to ensure you get back in one piece – there's a lot of planning, researching and form-filling to do (see the section on 'Travel facts').

Finding work for yourself

There's a surprisingly wide range of work available, depending on the length of time you want to spend abroad – for anything from a few weeks to a year. The Central Bureau for Educational Visits & Exchanges has 20 leaflets detailing the type of work available in various countries, including archaeology, au pairing, community work, conservation, fruit and vegetable picking, international work and peace camps, teaching and kibbutzim. The Bureau's excellent annually published information book, *Working Holidays*, gives specific details of organisations to write to, plus information about residence and work permits, health and insurance requirements etc. Write to the Bureau at Seymour Mews House, Seymour Mews, London W1H 9PE (telephone: 071-486 5101).

Other useful organisations:

The British Universities North America Club (BUNAC) enables students to work in countries (ie the USA) where work restrictions are normally prohibitive. The idea is to spend some time working and then using the money you've earned to travel around the country afterwards. BUNAC doesn't find you a job, but processes all the necessary paperwork to get your work application accepted in the USA or the other countries in the scheme (Canada, Jamaica and Australia). It's up to you to find your own job, either through the organisation's free job directory or your own personal contacts and initiative. You have pay your own travel expenses and prove you have adequate funds to support yourself while job-hunting (BUNAC can arrange loan facilities to fund you in the first instance).

If you're OK with kids and are reasonably sporty and outdoor by nature, why not consider applying for a job on that great American institution, the summer camp. BUNAC recruits counsellors in the UK via interviews which are held from November to the beginning of May. The earlier you apply, the better chance you have of obtaining a placement. If you're successful, your air fare is paid for you (but deducted from your earnings), and you get free board and lodging while you're working, plus up to six weeks at the end for holidaying. For more information, write to BUNAC, 16 Bowling Green Lane, London EC1R 0BD (telephone: 071-251 3472).

GAP Activity Projects

If you want to travel and do something useful and totally rewarding in your year off, then as a GAP volunteer you could find yourself teaching English as a foreign language, caring for the sick, handicapped and deprived, working in a school or helping on a farm or a conservation project.

143

Each year more than 750 volunteers are placed in 30 different countries (foreign GAP volunteers come to the UK too) for periods varying from six to nine months. In particular, there are increasing opportunities for voluntary work in eastern European countries such as Poland, Hungary, Russia, the Czech Republic, Slovakia and Bulgaria.

Volunteers are carefully selected, and are required to pay a GAP fee (the organisation is a registered charity), return air fare, medical, insurance and visa expenses and, if teaching English, the cost of a TEFL course before departure.

The closing date for applications is 1st February each year, but you're advised to get your application in early in the first term of your final school year because interviews begin in October and many places are filled by February.

For more information, write to GAP Activity Projects (GAP) Limited, GAP House, 44 Queen's Road, Reading, Berkshire RG1 4BB (telephone: 0734 594914).

TRAVEL FACTS

❏ Buy an International Student Identity Card (£5) and you're entitled to low cost travel in the form of special student prices on air, coach, rail and ferry fares around the world, plus student discounts on accommodation, sightseeing tours, museum and gallery admissions and entertainment.

❏ Plan your trips so that you can take advantage of fortune-saving travel passes such as Inter-Rail, Eurotrain Explorers and Amtrak Explorers. The Inter-Rail Europe pass allows you unlimited travel in 26 countries for one month for £249, plus discounts on many ferry and shipping services; while the Amtrak network pass allows you to travel across the USA coast to coast over 30 days for £167. For more information on these and numerous other money-saving travel concessions, contact the student travel specialists Campus Travel at 52 Grosvenor Gardens, London SW1W 0AG (telephone 071-730 2402/8111). There are also branches throughout the country.

❏ Before you depart, get to know as much as you can about each country you are visiting or passing through. Buy a good map and traveller's guide (see the section 'Useful reading' for suggestions). You can also get up-to-date information by contacting the Foreign Office (write to the Travel Advice Unit, Room CL 635, Consular Department, Petty France, London SW1H 9HD; telephone 071-270 4129).

❏ Use your common sense at all times, particularly regarding your own behaviour. Be sensitive to the moral and social attitudes of your host countries, and pay careful attention to the laws and penalties of each country. Britain is remarkably liberal in many respects, especially in attitudes to authority. So just because you're foreign, and a British student, don't make the mistake of assuming you are somehow exempt from respecting a country's laws and attitudes, regardless of whether you're in western Europe or much further afield. Ignorance or youth, almost invariably, is not accepted as an excuse.

❏ If you run out of money, don't be tempted to do anything illegal to raise some cash. In some countries acting as a drug courier can attract enormously long prison sentences – and even the death sentence. Always travel with a return ticket so that at least you have the means to get yourself home, and make the decision to return *before* you run into trouble. If you really get stuck, telephone home for help. Your parents should be able to arrange for money to be cabled to a local bank.

❏ If you're travelling around, you can save money on hotels etc by travelling on trains or coaches overnight. However, the time will come when your desire for clean sheets and a shower overrides your desire to economise. Up-to-date independent travel guides give excellent information on cheap and basic accommodation. Alternatively you can join the Youth Hostels Association and take and advantage of their 5,000-plus hostels worldwide (write to YHA National Office, Trevelyan House, 8 St Stephen's Hill, St Albans, Herts AL1 2DY; telephone 0727-5215). The YMCA and YWCA also have hostels throughout Europe and in the Middle East (write to the YWCA of Great Britain, Clarendon House, 52 Cornmarket Street, Oxford OX1 3EJ; telephone 0865 726110).

❏ Health-wise you're pretty safe in northern Europe, but further afield you will have to take various precautions. Two useful leaflets, SA40 *Before You Go* and SA41 *While You're Away*, tell you what and where. They're available from a DSS office or travel agent. Some countries require you to be immunised against specific diseases and to have a certificate as proof. Your doctor (or any commercial immunisation centre) can advise you on what's appropriate for where you're going, and give the necessary inoculations (for which you'll have to pay). Find out well in advance of your departure date just what's necessary. Some vaccines require a booster dose two or three weeks after the initial one, so you'll need to build this into your schedule.

❏ Adequate travel insurance is vital. If you're travelling in EC countries you are entitled to a certain amount of free or reduced rate medical treatment (obtain and complete form E111, available from post offices and DSS offices). However, you'd be advised to supplement this with private insurance. You will certainly need comprehensive insurance if you travel anywhere outside the EC. A policy should cover you for doctors' fees, the cost of medication, hospital fees, plus the cost of transporting you home by air ambulance (it has been known for parents to have to sell their homes to pay for bringing home a seriously ill child). The policy should also cover accidents, cancellations and loss, damage or theft of all your possessions.

Useful reading

You should find these books in your local library and in all good book shops. When you're travelling, limit yourself to one good all-round book.

Working Holidays, £6.95 (published by the Central Bureau for Educational Visits and Exchanges).

Travellers Survival Kit: Europe by David Woodworth, £6.95 (published by Vacation Work). Crucial, streetwise information for the independent traveller. Also in the series are guides to the Soviet Union and Eastern Europe, USA and Canada, Australia and New Zealand, the East and Cuba.

Eastern Europe/Mediterranean Europe/Western Europe/Scandinavian and Baltic Europe On A Shoestring, £10.75-£14.95 (published by Lonely Planet). Four travel guides for the independent traveller on a budget.

The Directory of Summer Jobs in Britain, £5.95 (Vacation Work).

The Directory of Summer Jobs Abroad, £5.95 (Vacation Work).

A Year Off, A Year On?, £5.95 (published by Hobsons Publishing in association with the Careers Research and Advisory Centre).

Hostelling International, Volumes 1,2 and 3, £5.99 each (published by the International Youth Hostel Federation).

Fielding's Budget Europe by Joseph and Judith Raff, £6.99 (Fielding and Morrow).

Europe on 10 Salads a Day by Mary Jane and Greg Edwards, £7.99 (Mustang Publishing). For the vegetarian traveller.

Cheap Sleep Guide to Europe by Katie Wood, £7.99 (Fontana).

Europe by Train by Katie Wood and George McDonald, £7.99 (Fontana).

PLUS check out the excellent country-by-country independent travel guides published by Fodor, Frommer and Rough Guides.

Chapter 10

STUDYING ABROAD

What you stand to gain – could you cope? – getting to know the language and customs – opportunities available to study – supporting yourself – practical arrangements – settling in

Once upon a time (not all that long ago either) it was only the lucky language student who could look forward to a period of studying overseas. Times have changed, and now countries from Argentina to Zaire are welcoming foreign students of all disciplines with open arms.

If you've ever pictured yourself wandering some foreign hall of Academe, there's no reason why you couldn't actually make it happen. The opportunities have never been greater, and it can even be quite straightforward to arrange, if, for example, your UK university has an exchange programme with other establishments overseas. However, you can also go the independent route and apply direct to universities in other countries yourself – provided you are prepared to devote a certain amount of time and persistence to the enterprise.

WHAT YOU STAND TO GAIN

Starting with the obvious, having spoken another language morning, noon and night, you'll be surprised how quickly you become fluent. Combine a language with other skills and you've got something that employers are increasingly on the look-out for as they extend their business networks around the globe.

You'll also gain an invaluable insight into another people – their culture and their ordinary daily life – which a lifetime of package holidays would never have revealed. In the process you'll become much more open-minded and tolerant, appreciative of other value systems and social attitudes.

You'll learn a lot about yourself, your strengths and your weaknesses – and you'll learn to deal with quite a few of the latter in the process. You'll also learn to stand on your own two feet under the most challenging circumstances, which should give you the self-confidence necessary to be enterprising in other areas of your life. It's the sort of experience that would impress a future employer, marking you out from the crowd of other hopefuls when you eventually launch yourself onto a competitive job market.

Do overseas qualifications count?

The experience of living in another culture, particularly the opportunity to really learn the language, may be motivation and justification enough for deciding to study abroad. However, you should also ask yourself how important it is that any qualification you receive is recognised in the UK. Degree courses in other countries tend to vary in content, duration and quality of qualification, although the EC is working on harmonising higher education to make it easier for students to study in other member countries and have qualifications gained in one recognised in the others. If you want to be certain that a particular overseas qualification will be recognised, contact the National Academic Recognition Information Centre at the British Council, 10 Spring Gardens, London SW1A 2BN (telephone 071-930 8466).

COULD YOU COPE WITH LIVING AND STUDYING IN A FOREIGN COUNTRY?

Any student who leaves home to study in another town has to cope with the challenges of independence and all that entails. But try and imagine what it would be like with the additional complications of another language and a foreign culture thrown in for good measure.

However strange your first few weeks are at college in the UK, at least you are surrounded by familiar, everyday things; magazines and newspapers, television and radio, your favourite brands of food, drink, shampoo etc. And should it prove too much for you, you can get on the coach or train and go home for the weekend for a little tender loving care.

You can't do that if you're living in another country – the cost would be prohibitive. And that alone can increase your sense of isolation. In the UK, to get the best of what life at university has to offer you have to be prepared to throw yourself whole-heartedly into college activities. It's exactly the same abroad, only more so. There's no point at all in contemplating studying in another country unless you're going to immerse yourself in its culture, get to know its people, eat its food and generally be prepared to do things its way.

If you're homesick, you have to pull yourself together and do something about it. If you're ill, you have to communicate your symptoms to a doctor in another language (it can be difficult enough doing it in English). If your toilet gets blocked you might have to get hold of and instruct a plumber – not to mention negotiate the bill (ditto).

If you're a shy, introverted kind of person who feels happier in a familiar environment, going off by yourself to live and study in a foreign country may be more than you can realistically cope with. If, however, you are outgoing, adaptable, reasonably self-reliant and eager for new experiences, you'll probably enjoy yourself so much that when the time comes for you to return home, you'll have to be forcibly dragged on to the plane.

FAMILIARISING YOURSELF WITH THE LANGUAGE AND THE COUNTRY

If you're considering studying in a non-English speaking country, is your command of the language up to it? You may be reasonably confident conversing at a social level, but being able to understand and discuss complex academic concepts and write essays and dissertations to an adequate standard require a more thorough facility with a language. Not being proficient is bound to increase any sense of isolation you may be feeling being away from home, and will leave you floundering academically. For this reason, most universities or educational institutions will insist on a foreign student undergoing a proficiency examination before being considered for admission to a course. You can, of course, brush up on the language in preparation, and you may even be eligible for a grant to help you finance an intensive course (see later section).

You will also stand a better chance of settling in and taking culture shock in your stride if you have researched the country thoroughly beforehand.

❏ Speak to people who've travelled (rather than simply holidayed) or better still, worked there, and find out what the drawbacks are as well as the good things.

❏ If possible, get hold of some newspapers or magazines and familiarise yourself with current events, popular issues and personalities.

❏ Find out as much as you can about the way people conduct their daily lives (when they eat meals, how formal/informal they are socially and so on).

❏ Find out about their attitudes and likely opinions to such matters as authority, religion, politics, moral and social issues. This is especially important because the last thing you want to do is to cause offence by unwittingly bringing up taboo subjects or making inappropriate remarks.

❏ Learn all you can about etiquette, the subtle nuances as well as the more obvious aspects. Do you, for example, bring a gift if you're invited to someone's home, and if so, what would be suitable?

❏ Find out what you can about the country's laws, and the penalties for breaking them (some countries take a strict line on things that wouldn't raise an eyebrow in Britain, such as jaywalking or crossing the road before the little green man lights up). Don't make the mistake of assuming that because you're a foreigner you're exempt from your host country's laws and standards of behaviour.

OPPORTUNITIES FOR STUDYING ABROAD

The opportunities for studying overseas are increasing all the time as a result of excellent initiatives by the EC and a willingness shared by many countries to promote cultural, technological and educational exchanges.

There are a variety of routes available, depending on where and what you want to study, and for how long. You can opt for a few weeks at a language school during the summer vacation, spend up to a year at a university, or even study for a complete degree.

The easiest route is to find out if your UK college has an exchange scheme already in existence with an overseas college which you could take part in. Otherwise you can research and draw up your own shortlist of possible universities and apply direct yourself. There are several directories and handbooks which you can use to help you in your search, most of them should be available in your local library. Some are listed below. Be prepared for the procedure to take a lot of time, especially if you want to study a full degree, and a great deal of paperwork and administration.

Direct enrolment at an overseas college

You can take a year out from your UK degree course (with your college's permission) and enrol as a visiting student at an overseas university, although it won't contribute towards your UK qualification. You can enrol direct yourself by writing to a university of your choice. The following publications list names and addresses of universities and education institutions around the world, plus lots of other invaluable information and advice. Copies should be available in your local library.

How To Study Abroad by Teresa Tinsley (published by Northcote House Publishers)

Higher Education in the European Community – A Student Handbook (published by Kogan Page)

Applying to Colleges and Universities in the United States – a handbook for international students (published by Peterson's Guides)

Commonwealth Universities Year Book (published by the Association of Commonwealth Universities)

Directory of Work and Study in Developing Countries (Vacation Work Publications)

European Council of International Schools Higher Education Directory (Published by ECIS)

The European Community Action Scheme for the Mobility of University Students (ERASMUS)

University students of member countries can elect to spend up to a year at an EC university as a recognised part of their 'home' degree course. ERASMUS funds these joint study programmes (see the section on finance), and to be eligible you should be enrolled at a university or college of higher education in the UK that takes part in the scheme. When you're considering your applications to individual UK universities and colleges, find out first if they are in the scheme. You can also contact ERASMUS direct for a list of the participating EC universities (write to The UK ERASMUS Students Grant Council, The University, Canterbury, Kent CT2 7PD; telephone 0227-762712).

The International Association for the Exchange of Students for Technical Experience (IAESTE)

This is an exchange scheme administered at the UK end by the Vocational and Technical Education department of the Central Bureau for Educational Visits and Exchanges. Science and technology students are given work experience relevant to their course in one of over 50 participating countries, including Eastern Europe. For more information write to the Bureau at Seymour Mews, London W1H 9PE (telephone 071-486 5101).

The International Association of Students of Economics and Business (AIESEC)

An exchange scheme offering overseas traineeships to students or recent graduates in these disciplines. For more information write to AIESEC at The Central Bureau for Educational Visits and Exchanges.

English Language Assistants Programme

This is a scheme co-ordinated by the Central Bureau for Educational Visits and Exchanges enabling students and recent graduates of modern languages to spend approximately nine months teaching English at an educational institution overseas (26 countries participate in the scheme). For more information, write to the Bureau.

Learning a language on a study holiday

If you want to learn a European language from scratch, or bring an existing one up to a fluent and idiomatic standard, you can enrol on a study course in your chosen country for a period of anything between three and 300 days. Information on the courses available can be found in the Central Bureau of Educational Visits and Exchanges' own publication, *Study Holidays*, price £9.45, and available by post from the address above.

FINANCING YOUR STAY

First of all you have to find out exactly what it's going to cost you, and then if there are any grants you might be eligible for. You may, for example, have to pay tuition fees, and also examination and registration fees. Confirm this with your college. You will almost certainly have to pay for your accommodation, and you'll have to budget for your return plane, train or coach fare. Expect to fork for the following as well: books and stationery; student membership/club membership fees; daily travel and food expenses; entertainment; immigration /exit surcharges.

☐ If you're spending a term or so abroad as part of a UK degree course then your LEA will continue to pay your grant for that period and may even top it up further if you're studying in a country where living costs are high. You will also get help with your travelling expenses.

☐ If your course is approved under the ERASMUS programme you may be eligible for a top-up grant towards the cost studying abroad, including travel expenses, the cost of a language course beforehand and general living costs.

☐ If you're studying a foreign language in an EC country for between three months and a year you may be eligible for a top-up grant under the LINGUA programme, which promotes the teaching and learning of EC languages by offering grants and other support. For more information contact LINGUA at The Central Bureau for Educational Visits and Exchanges (address as above).

☐ Another EC scheme, TEMPUS (Trans-European Mobility Scheme for University Studies), offers financial assistance for students studying at a university for a period in an approved central or eastern European country. For more information write to TEMPUS, British Council, Medlock Street, Manchester M15 4PR (telephone 061-957 7000).

☐ The European Community Action Programme for Education and Training for Technology (COMETT) promotes links between universities and industry and provides scholarships for individuals. Contact the COMETT Liaison Office, Department for Education, Sanctuary Buildings, Great Smith Street, London SW1P 3BT (telephone 071-925 5254).

There are other are other sources of finance available through scholarships, bursaries and grants, information about which you can find in the following publications (they should be available in your local reference library):

The Grant Register (published by Macmillan Press).

Study Abroad XXVI (published by UNESCO). Lists more than 200,000 scholarships, fellowships, assistantships and travel grants at universities throughout the world. (£14, available direct from HMSO Publications Centre, PO Box 276, London SW8 5DT.)

Studying Abroad (published by the British Council, 10 Spring Gardens, London SW1A 2BN). Provides information on scholarships (for an academic year) and bursaries (for shorter periods) being offered by overseas governments and universities.

Higher Education in the European Community: Student Handbook (published by Kogan Page, available from HMSO Publications, as above, £13.95). Contains invaluable information for anyone considering studying abroad, including information on available grants.

Study Holidays (published by the Central Bureau for Educational Visits and Exchanges). Information on language courses, plus grants, scholarships and bursaries.

PRACTICAL CONSIDERATIONS BEFORE YOU DEPART

Once you've been accepted on a course you have a number of practical arrangements to take care of. If your overseas studies are an accredited part of a UK course, your college may be able to help you with some of the necessary paperwork.

Immigration requirements

Depending on where you'll be studying and how long for, you may require a visa and/or a resident's permit. You'll also need a current full British passport (not a visitor's passport). You can obtain the necessary information and forms from the country's embassy or consulate, but allow plenty of time as it can take a while to process the documentation. If you need a new British passport, this can also take some time to process.

The immigration department may also require other information, including (a) evidence from your overseas college that you have been accepted on a course and (b) evidence that you will be able to support yourself financially for the duration of your stay.

Finding somewhere to live

Try and sort this out before you leave the UK, as arriving without a place to stay isn't a great introduction to a new country. Somewhere in all the information sent by the college there should be details on accommodation. If the college has its own, apply for a place as soon as possible (you may be given priority as a foreign student). If it doesn't, ask the college to advise you on the best way of finding your own accommodation.

If you have no other option but to look for somewhere when you arrive, the local tourist information centre should be able to recommend a hostel or inexpensive hotel. It may not be ideal, but you can use it as a base to find somewhere more suitable. Then check out college noticeboards, local newspapers and anything else likely to advertise rooms for rent. You should also find out if there's a YMCA or YWCA in the town or city. These are very popular with foreign students because they are reasonably priced and generally have excellent facilities. Contact the YMCA of Great Britain, Clarendon House, 52 Cornmarket Street, Oxford, OX1 3EJ (telephone: 0865-7226110).

Insurance

If you fall sick or have an accident while you're abroad you will have to pay for any emergency medical treatment you receive. Some countries (the EC member countries for example) have a reciprocal arrangement with the UK and will provide limited treatment free or at a reduced cost. You need to take with you a copy of form E111 (available from a post office or DSS office), which lists the countries participating in the scheme, and also explains what to do if you have to make a claim, and what treatment is free or available at a reduced cost. You should also take out supplementary insurance.

There are countries (eg the USA) where free or subsidised medical treatment is unavailable, and it's therefore imperative that you take out a comprehensive insurance plan to cover you for doctor's fees, the cost of medication, hospital fees and the cost of transporting you home by air ambulance.

Your insurance policy should also cover you for accidents, death, cancellations of travel plans and loss, damage or theft of your possessions.

Vaccinations

Find out if there are any vaccination requirements, and arrange to have what's necessary in good time (sometimes booster shots are needed two or three weeks after the initial treatment). In countries where malaria is endemic you must take medication with you and be sure to take it as prescribed. Some vaccinations are mandatory outside northern Europe, but ask your doctor's advice on whether you should have additional protection against diseases such as polio and hepatitis.

Travel arrangements

Once your place is confirmed you will have to start thinking about how you're going to get there. You may have to book in advance if you're likely to be travelling in a peak holiday period to make sure you arrive on time for enrolment, and also to get the best deal on ticket prices.

Think carefully about what you're going to take with you. Unless you want to go to the bother of sending a trunk-full of your possessions on ahead (expensive and not worth it unless you're going for a considerable period), you'll be effectively limited by what you can physically carry – probably no more than a couple of suitcase-loads. That means you'll really only have room for clothes (find out

how what sort of weather and seasons you can expect to encounter), a few favourite books and maybe a bedside picture to
remind you of home. Don't take anything of real value as you
won't have any idea how secure your accommodation is until you
get there.

Money

Obviously you're going to need access to money during your stay,
so you need to work out how you're going to get your funds there
as inexpensively and as conveniently as possible. Ask your bank
for advice, and allow plenty of time to set up a suitable arrangement. If you're there for some time, it could be more convenient to
open a bank account locally. Transferring money from one country
to another doesn't always work smoothly however well you think
you've planned it, so you'd be advised to take a credit card or
some travellers cheques to tide you over the first couple of weeks
in case you run into problems.

SETTLING IN WHEN YOU ARRIVE

If you can, arrive a few days before your course begins so that you
can settle into your accommodation (or get something organised if
you haven't done so in advance of your arrival). It also gives you a
chance to get out and about and get your bearings – play the
tourist a little – so that you begin to get a feel for the place. Buy a
good street map and walk as much as possible. Find out also how
to use the train, underground, bus or tram systems, and what sort
of tickets are the most convenient and economic. As part of your
explorations, go and find the college, and then work out a practical
route for getting there. On your first day you will be expected to
officially register at the college or university, and meet the lecturers
and other students in your department.

Colleges abroad operate similarly to British ones, in that there is
usually a student organisation and a variety of sports and social
clubs. See what your college has to offer, and make a point of joining a couple of clubs so that you start getting out and meeting people. Some colleges may even have a club for foreign students.

Don't be too surprised if you feel a bit homesick to begin with, as
no matter how well you prepare yourself in advance, things are

bound to seem very different to what you had expected, and to what you've been used to back at home. Soon, as you learn the ropes, find your way round, become more confident in the language and start to collect friends, you'll grow more and more at home. Before you know it, you'll feel as though you've lived there all your life!

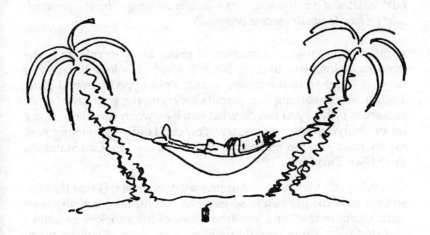

Chapter 11

ENJOYING YOUR INDEPENDENCE

Making new relationships – dealing with lecherous lecturers – sexual harassment and date rape – looking after your health – contraception – HIV, AIDS and practising safe sex – healthy drinking – drugs – personal safety – how to handle obscene phonecalls

Arguably the greatest attraction of going away to college is the freedom, at long last, to enjoy life, relationships, a long lie-in – you name it – free from the disapproving, tight-lipped parental gaze. There really is nothing like parents for cramping your style! Once you are at college you can do what you like, when you like – even a bit of studying when necessary. You can boldly go seeking new experiences. You can make your own mistakes. You Can Stand On Your Own Two Feet.

One thing you may not have appreciated, however, is that the constraints of home life you're so eager to cast off have actually been quite useful in shielding you from some of life's trickier situations and decisions. Consequently there may be times at college when you find yourself in an awkward or uncomfortable situation and you're not sure how to deal with it. This chapter isn't meant to be some sort of companion piece to the long list of 'dos and don'ts' that your parents will undoubtedly have prepared for you (they mean well, bless them!). What it does do is outline some of the more obvious pitfalls, and also provide information that could be useful so that you are able to make up your own mind how to deal with specific situations, should they arise.

MAKING NEW RELATIONSHIPS

Sexual attitudes are more liberal at college but paradoxically this can become a pressure, too. It's probably a good idea to take things easy in your first few weeks, and make establishing a circle of friends more of a priority than finding a new girlfriend or boyfriend.

When you do meet someone you fancy you may be uncertain how things should proceed, especially if it's your first big relationship. The most important thing is to take your time and get to know someone. The most rewarding (and often most lasting) relationships tend to start from a basis of mutual trust, friendship and shared interests. Don't feel pressured to rush into a sexual relationship, especially if it's the first real one for either of you. Despite the impressions they may seek to give you, not everyone is busy having affairs left, right and centre.

Two useful things to remember. One: your new-found freedom to say 'yes' to new experiences gives you equal freedom to say 'no'. Two: those who brag loudest about their sex lives usually have the least to brag about.

LEAVING SOMEONE BEHIND

It's a bit of a wrench leaving behind your friends from home, but at least most of them are college-bound too, and you'll be able to meet up in the vacations. It can be much more difficult leaving behind your girlfriend or boyfriend.

You're going to miss each other a lot, there's no denying that. The difference is that while you're busy making new friends, having a great social life and filling in any leftover moments with a spot of studying, your partner will be carrying on much as usual, without the distraction of a new lifestyle to take his or her mind off your absence. Separation invariably puts a strain on a relationship, and you could find pressure being put on you in all sorts of ways; to come home most weekends – maybe even to come home permanently.

Be sympathetic, but be firm as well. Above all, don't give in to moral blackmail. Your relationship is important, but so also are your studies and all the other opportunities university has to offer. If it's a good and a strong relationship, it will survive your time apart.

Before you leave for college, reassure your partner that you'll keep regularly in touch through letters and telephone calls and then stick to your promises. Arrange to go home for the occasional weekend, but not too frequently or your social life at college will suffer too. If it's convenient, invite your partner to come and stay with you; she/he might find being apart a little easier given some idea of the life you lead at college – and that long hours of studying is a major part!

Don't forget your parents may miss you too

Leaving parents behind can be a wrench as well, especially if you are an only child or your parent is widowed or divorced. Again, you can find yourself subjected to pressure to come home more weekends than perhaps you had in mind. The way to handle the situation is much as described above; write and telephone regularly, and give your parent(s) a date to look forward to when you'll be home for a weekend.

It's only natural for a parent to want and come and see your new environment, but inviting a parent to actually stay with you can be tricky for all sorts of reasons. If you're living in a hall of residence, for example, you're unlikely to have the facilities to put someone up. It won't necessarily be any easier if you're sharing a flat, either (and you'd have to get the permission from your flatmates). Depending on the length of the journey, it may be more practical to invite your parent up for the day rather than an overnight stay.

AVOIDING THE LECHEROUS LECTURER

You can't help who you fall for, but having said that, you'll save yourself a great deal of embarrassment and heartache if you avoid having a relationship with a lecturer.

University authorities tend to view such situations unfavourably – some are even thinking of banning student/lecturer relationships altogether. And they have good reason, too. When you're new to college life it's easy to be flattered by the attentions of someone who's older and seemingly successful in the academic world. Unfortunately, there will always be some lecturers – male and female – who take advantage of their position in this respect. From your point of view, a relationship with a lecturer can lead to all sorts of awkwardnesses, not least if he/she is responsible for assessing your coursework. It wouldn't be unnatural, for example, for your coursemates to think you're getting special treatment – and that would affect your relationship with them.

SEXUAL HARASSMENT

Relationships between men and women, both social and sexual, are more relaxed and liberated these days, but that doesn't mean that anything goes. There remain certain basic rules of etiquette (good manners is another way of putting it) to be observed whether you're in college, at work, relaxing with a group of friends or out on a date.

Much of the misunderstanding between men and women occurs because somebody doesn't understand, or maybe doesn't even know, the rules. If you've spent the last few years at a single sex school or a boarding or public school you may not have had much opportunity to learn them. Knowing the rules isn't everything – although it does mean you're less likely to make a fool of yourself or embarrass someone else. You have to use your judgement to decide when a friendship is ready to be put on a more relaxed or a more intimate footing. Usually these things happen naturally by a mutual understanding. Somebody's got to make a move after all – or nothing will ever happen. A least by that time you probably know enough about a person to be pretty certain how he or she is likely to respond.

Sexual harassment often occurs because the 'harasser' is either oblivious to the rules or has badly misjudged the situation. It's less likely to occur among friends, but can be quite common in work situations and even institutions like universities and colleges. Women are usually (though not exclusively) the victims, often because they are in a so-called subordinate position (ie boss/secretary, lecturer/student).

What should you do if you're harassed?

Doing anything can be difficult if you're worried that a lecturer might make trouble for you, or that you might lose your precious part-time job at a restaurant if you tell your boss where to get off.

If you have been verbally or physically sexually harassed you don't have to suffer in silence. More and more universities and colleges are taking a tough line against harassment, whether by lecturers or other students. You should be able to speak in confidence to your personal tutor (unless he/she is the perpetrator), but it might be a better idea to talk to your student union's welfare officer or women's officer, as they will have more experience in dealing with such matters. They can also advise you on the official complaints procedure.

Keep a record of the time and dates of events, including what was done and said. If possible, have a witness. Often a formal reprimand by the college authorities will put a stop to such behaviour, and the fact that it's a matter of record will lessen the chances of your being 'punished' through poor essay marks or whatever for having reported your harasser. If stronger action is deemed necessary and someone's job or college place is at risk, you will have to be very sure of your facts and prepared to put up with potentially a great deal of unpleasantness – even though you are the victim.

Date rape

No one would deny that rape is a dreadful experience for any woman – or man – to go through, so why does the phenomenon of 'date rape' cause particular controversy? Part of the reason may be that very little is actually known about date rape because few women (the most likely victims) report it when it happens to them.

It's been suggested that this may be because the actual circumstances weren't absolutely clear in the victim's mind.

If you're attacked in the street by a stranger or someone you know uses physical force and fear to make you have sex with them, that's rape. But what if you had a few drinks and you go back to your boyfriend's room and end up having sex? You may not have intended or want to have sex, but suddenly things start to get intimate, your boyfriend gets 'carried away', you try and protest but before you know it, things had reached the point of no return and you didn't know how to stop it. Was that rape?

The answer is: yes, it was, if you genuinely didn't want sex and you feel you were coerced into it – but you can imagine the difficulties of having to try and explain the actual circumstances to the college authorities or a police officer. That not only did you invite your alleged attacker back to your room but were initially happy enough to cuddle up on the sofa together. Rape can be difficult and humiliating enough to prove, without clouding the issue and giving your attacker a potential advantage in court (the sort of thing elderly male judges take great satisfaction in calling 'contributory negligence').

For the record, sexual etiquette decrees that (a) a woman sets the pace and (b) she has the right to say no to sex, right up to the point of penetration. But imagine just for a moment how frustrating that must be for a man, fired up and ready to go. That's not an argument for going ahead and having sex under duress. It is, however, an argument for women taking common sense measures to avoid getting themselves into such a situation in the first place.

LOOKING AFTER YOUR HEALTH

Contrary to what the outside world may think, a student's life can be pretty stressful. There's the constant pressure of essay deadlines, revision and exams and trying to make ends meet on an inadequate income – and wondering if there'll be a job waiting for you at the end of it all. New students have even more to cope with in the first few weeks and months as they get to grips with a new environment, new friends, new course and masses of new experiences – all without the reassuring support of family and friends.

A certain amount of stress is good for you. It's what makes life exciting. It's what helps you pull out the stops to get things (like essays and revision) done. It's what gives you the push and determination to succeed – at your studies, on the football field, in your future career.

Your ability to use stress as a positive thing in your life depends to a great degree on your health and general well-being, and in getting the right balance between working and having fun. You are at college to study for a degree, which may be crucial to your future career plans. But you're also at college to explore opportunities you've never had before – or may have again. And the wonderful thing about opportunities is that you never know where they're going to lead you. Joining the debating society could prove the catalyst for a career in politics (as it has for so many), the dramatics society for a life on the boards, the college Judo team for a medal at the next Olympics, a spell raising money for local charities via Rag Week for a lifetime's fulfilling work with Save the Children.

Establishing a manageable study routine which leaves you feeling on top of your work and with time to relax and have fun is your first priority, once Freshers Week is over. So is settling into a 'personal maintenance' routine; adequate sleep, regular exercise, a reasonably healthy and varied diet. There'll be times when you want to play hard – why not, if you work hard? But compensate with a week off the booze, a couple of early nights or whatever else is appropriate.

CONTRACEPTION

When you go to bed with your boyfriend or girlfriend, one of you should be using some form of contraception. Traditionally this responsibility has fallen to the female partner, and that's not necessarily a bad thing. As she is the one with the most to risk if there's an unwanted pregnancy she may feel happier and more confident being responsible for taking the precautions. That said, in this liberated day and age there's no reason why a man can't take responsibility with his partner's agreement. And there's no excuse at all for him to assume, without bothering to ask, that his partner is taking precautions.

There are several forms of contraception available, and your GP or family planning clinic at the campus health centre will help you to decide which is likely to suit you and your circumstances best. The following are the most reliable and widely used methods. Whichever method you decide to use, you should also use a condom every time you make love as a safeguard against contracting a sexually transmitted disease. Just why this is so important is explained later in this chapter under the section about safer sex.

If you or your partner do become pregnant, either because you've had unprotected sex or for some reason your contraception has failed, Chapter 12, 'Help', explains what you can do about the situation.

Oral contraceptives (The Pill): The most commonly used pill is the combined pill, which consists of two hormones, oestrogen and progestogen, which prevent the release of an egg into the uterus each month. You take the pill for 21 days, and then have a seven day break, during which time you have a light period. The pill doesn't suit everybody; some women experience side effects, others are unlikely to have it prescribed if they are overweight, smoke heavily or over the age of 35. The combined pill is currently the most effective form of contraceptive.

The mini pill contains no oestrogen at all and usually a smaller amount of progestogen than the combined pill. It has fewer side effects as well, and is often prescribed as an alternative for women who can't take the combined version. It acts differently from the combined pill in that it stops an estimated one in two eggs passing into the uterus, and it thickens the mucus at the uterus's neck, preventing sperm from reaching the egg. The one practical drawback of the mini pill is that it has to be taken every single day at the same time (there's about an hour's leeway either side). In other words, you need to be a pretty disciplined sort of person, otherwise you could risk an unplanned pregnancy.

Diaphragms and caps: These are shallow plastic or rubber domes which are smeared with spermicide and then inserted in the vagina and over the cervix (the neck of the uterus) before intercourse, and left in place for several hours afterwards. A diaphragm/cap does two things. It keeps sperm from getting to the egg and it keeps the spermicide in place.

Diaphragms and caps are available in different sizes, and have to be professionally fitted to make sure the size is correct, and the first-time user is also shown how to insert it properly. These devices have almost no side effects, although some women find them a bit messy to use, and they can affect the spontaneity of love-making.

Condoms: These are very thin rubber sheaths which are rolled on to an erect penis just before vaginal intercourse starts. The sperm is prevented from entering the vagina, and remains in the condom, which is then disposed of. A condom has to be handled carefully (otherwise it could split), and it's important to use good quality brands that bear the British Standard kite mark. Failure in any of these respects seriously affects the condom's reliability. Condoms have no side effects, and are very effective at protecting against sexually transmitted diseases and cancer of the cervix.

Intra-uterine devices (IUDs) or coils: These are long plastic devices about one and a half inches in length which are profession-ally inserted in the vagina and left in place for a period of about a year. Somehow (no one knows for sure) they prevent a fertilised egg from developing. However, because there could be a small risk of pelvic infection which in turn could result in infertility, family planning clinics don't as a rule prescribe the use of a IUD or coil for women of child-bearing age who haven't completed their families.

HIV AND AIDS

Human Immunodeficiency Virus (HIV) is the virus that causes AIDS. You can have HIV and lead a healthy life for many years before developing AIDS. You can also pass the virus on to others – unwittingly, if you don't know you've got it in the first place.

HIV is transmitted in three main ways: through unprotected sexual intercourse (either vaginal or anal); by drug-users sharing needles and other equipment; from an infected mother to her baby either before or during birth or through breast-feeding. HIV is not passed through ordinary everyday things like kissing, hugging, coughing, sneezing or sharing kitchen or toilet facilities.

The groups most at risk from HIV and AIDS are male homosexuals who don't practise safe sex (or haven't done so in the past) and intravenous drug-users of either gender. But don't make the mis-take of thinking you're safe if you're not in one of these groups. It can happen to anyone. It could happen the first time you have sex if your partner is infected and you don't use a condom.

What is safer sex?

Whether you are heterosexual or gay, you can greatly reduce your chances of becoming infected with HIV – or any other sexually transmitted disease such as thrush, genital herpes, gonorrhoea or non-specific urethritis – if you avoid sleeping around and if you and your partner use a condom every time you make love (even if you are using another form of contraception).

It's a good idea to keep a condom accessible (either in a jacket pocket or a drawer beside your bed), as it's in the heat of passion that people are particularly vulnerable to risking unsafe sex. These days it's perfectly acceptable for a woman as well as a man to carry condoms – then at least one of you is prepared. Having sex for the first time with a new partner can be a bit tricky, though. The best tack is probably to be matter-of-fact and produce the condom at the appropriate moment. Your partner may well be relieved at not having to be the one to raise the subject. And if he or she objects, do insist; after all it's your health that's potentially at risk.

You can get supplies of condoms from your college's family planning clinic. They are also available from vending machines in lavatories in pubs and clubs, and your college's men's and women's toilets. You can also buy condoms from chemists and pharmacists, supermarkets and many grocers. They're usually sold on a self-service basis, so there's no embarrassment involved.

What to do if you're worried about AIDS

Speak to your doctor, who will treat you in the strictest confidence, and won't pass on information to the university authorities without your express consent. Alternatively you can call the National Aids Helpline on 0800-567 123. Calls are free and confidential, and help is available 24 hours a day, seven days a week.

If you think you may have been put at risk, you can ask for a blood test, which will show whether or not you have the virus. You may be asked to wait at least three months before having the test because the HIV antibodies can take two to three months from the time of infection to appear in the bloodstream.

Before you finally go ahead with the test, your doctor or counsellor will want to make sure you understand the implications of knowing you have HIV. Some people prefer not to know for certain because there's still always the possibility that they don't have the virus. On the other hand, if you do know you can start receiving treatment which may delay the progress of the virus and the onset of AIDS itself. You can also take precautions so you don't pass the virus on to anyone else.

Knowing you have HIV has other consequences. You can't predict how your parents, family and friends will react until you tell them. You will also, in the future, have major difficulties getting a mortgage and life insurance.

There are self help groups who can help and advise you through these and any other problems you come across.

ALCOHOL

The lure of cheap booze at the student union bar, excessive socialising in Freshers Week and the quite understandable need for a confidence-boosting drink while you try to create a new circle of friends from scratch – all these mean that you might find yourself knocking it back a bit in your first few weeks at university.

As you settle into college life your alcohol intake should settle down, too. Anyway, even at the subsidised prices of your hall or student union bar, it's an expensive pastime that your grant certainly doesn't cater for. Keep any drinking to evenings, after you've finished studying, and then don't overdo it – especially if you have a nine o'clock lecture or exam next morning.

Keeping your drinking at a safe level:
doctors recommend a maximum limit of
21 units for men and 14 units for
women, spread over a
week (don't save up
your allowance

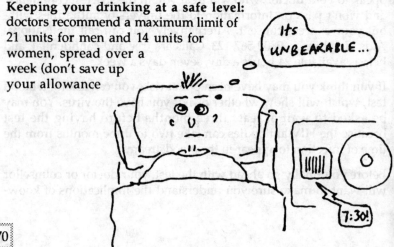

for a mega-binge on Saturday night). A unit represents half a pint of beer or lager, a small glass of wine or a single measure of spirits. If you drink more than this on a regular basis you could be doing long term damage to your health.

Dealing with a hangover: however moderate a drinker you are, there is bound to come a time (celebrating the end of exams, perhaps) when you overdo things outrageously and end up feeling so ill you'd really quite like to die. While a lot of people have their pet cures, when you're in the throes of a hangover there's not a great deal you can do to make things better, beyond drinking fresh fruit juice (the Vitamin C is supposed to be beneficial) and taking a couple of paracetamol tablets (not aspirin, it will irritate the stomach lining and will make you feel queasier than ever). Throwing up can help, too.

If you know you're going to be drinking, you can take some precautions to help lessen the symptoms of a hangover. Having something to eat (or a large glass of milk) beforehand can delay the absorption of alcohol into the bloodstream.

Watch what type of alcohol you drink as well, and don't mix your drinks. All alcoholic drinks contain substances called *congeners*, which are responsible for producing the side effects associated with a hangover. Some drinks give you more of a hangover than others because they have more congeners. Vodka, gin and white wine, for instance, have comparatively few, while brandy has loads, along with red wine, bourbon, rum and sherry. Beer and Scotch whisky are about middling. Cheap wines tend to have more congeners than better quality wines.

If you do overdo it, you can lessen the intensity of the side effects provided you act before you go to bed. Making yourself sick can help get rid of any alcohol still in the stomach before it has a chance to get absorbed. Drinking as much water as you comfortably can (ie about a pint) can slow down the dehydration caused by too much alcohol.

If you think you have a problem: it could affect your relationships and your studies, so pluck up your courage to ask for help. And it does take courage to ask for help, which is why you'll be treated with respect and in confidence. You won't be treated in a judgmental, tut-tutting way. You can get help and advice from your college or student union welfare officer. You can also contact Alcoholics

Anonymous, either by looking them up in the telephone directory or by calling them on 0904-644026 (you'll be put in touch with a local group in your area). It may also be a good idea to confide in your personal tutor, who can liaise on your behalf with course lecturers if your studies have suffered as a result of your drinking.

DRUGS

The term 'illegal drug' refers to the taking of any drug that's not available on prescription or over the pharmacy counter. People start taking drugs for three main reasons: because it makes them feel good; to feel part of a group in which it's being offered around; or because they're worried about being thought boring if they don't.

There are sound reasons for not getting involved in taking illegal drugs. While the initial high may be pleasant, some drugs (eg heroin and crack) are highly addictive, and some (eg amphetamine, crack, cocaine and ecstasy) can lead to tolerance and the need for larger doses. The inevitable 'down' afterwards can become increasingly disturbing, and can include sleeplessness, paranoia, tiredness and depression.

If you are caught in possession of an illegal drug you could be risking a fine, being kicked out of college, even imprisonment. Drugs can cause serious secondary problems. Supporting a habit can be very expensive, and addicts frequently have to turn to crime to raise money. Impurely processed drugs can cause deeply unpleasant side effects, even death. And sharing a needle or other equipment when injecting intravenously puts the user at serious risk of contracting the HIV virus, and ultimately AIDS.

The best thing is to avoid drugs altogether. This is especially important if you have a heart condition of any kind, or if you (or anyone in your family) has a history of psychological or psychiatric problems.

You'll hear claims that cannabis is harmless, and no worse than alcohol. While it's true that cannabis is probably the safest of the illegal drugs, it can have serious side-effects – including all the problems associated with smoking tobacco – depending on how much and how regularly it's taken. And, just like alcohol, it can affect your ability and motivation to study, and also to drive and operate machinery.

If you think you have a problem with drugs: your college or student union welfare officer will be able to give you confidential help and advice on how to tackle it. Alternatively you can telephone Release, the national drugs and legal helpline, on 071-603 8654. The service is available 24 hours and totally confidential.

PERSONAL SAFETY

University authorities and student unions take personal safety very seriously – and so should you. While anybody can be the victim of a mugging or a burglary, women students are considered especially vulnerable. Consequently more and more colleges run special bus services at night, organise self-defence courses and most, if not all, provide women students with free or discounted rape alarms. Some colleges are even organising their own student-run security patrols to help make their campuses safer.

Although women are traditionally regarded as the more likely targets of assault, it's young men who have been shown, statistically, to be the greater victims, largely as a result of drinking too much and then getting into arguments and fights. There has also been an increase in the incidence of male rape (by other males) in recent years.

The point of this section isn't to get the wind up you, so you never venture out during your time at college. Like the presenter says on the BBC1's regular crime series: don't have nightmares – the majority of people never experience a criminal event of any sort. The point of this section is to show you how you can minimise risk and, equally important, increase your confidence, by using your common sense and following a few basic precautions. Forewarned is forearmed, as the saying goes – whatever your gender.

When you're out and about

Attackers prefer soft targets, so don't make yourself look vulnerable. Walk with a confident, purposeful step and always pay full attention to your surroundings, especially in areas or situations where you think you may be vulnerable. Get into the habit of carrying your keys, travel pass or ticket and some change in a coat or jacket pocket, so that in the unlikely event of your being mugged (a) you can still get yourself home and (b) you at least won't have to worry about your attacker being able to gain entrance to your home or having to have your locks changed – a very expensive procedure.

☐ Use your common sense and don't take unnecessary risks. Stick to well-lit roads and as far as possible avoid shortcuts via dark alleys or unlit open spaces (admittedly not always easy, given the design of many campuses). Walk facing oncoming traffic, and on the outer side of the pavement, away from dark doorways and alleys. Be aware of parked vehicles which could be concealing attackers.

☐ If you use public transport, especially late at night, try to travel with a friend. Wait for buses at stops on busy roads, preferably ones with a queue. Try not to rely on night buses, which are too few and far between; instead club together with friends and share the cost of a taxi home. Don't go on the top deck of buses, but try to sit near the driver. If you're travelling on a train or an underground system, always get into a carriage that has plenty of people; if the one you're in empties, move to another more crowded one.

☐ If you need to use a cab, always use an official one, or telephone a reliable cab company. Always check the driver's credentials – ask him to tell you which company he's from. If you're walking along the street and a car stops claiming to be a mini-cab *do not get in*. Apart from the fact that it's illegal for mini-cabs to ply for hire, your would-be rescuer could be some sort of pervert, on the look-out for vulnerable-looking individuals.

☐ Get into the habit of doing things in the company of friends. Go to parties or the cinema in a small group. After a late lecture, meet up with one of your flatmates or a friend at hall and travel home together. When you go out alone to meet up with friends, agree to meet in a public place. Always let someone know where you're off to, and roughly what time you'll be getting back.

☐ If you feel uneasy or think you are being followed listen to your instinct. You still have time to avoid a confrontation. Resist the temptation to walk faster or keep looking behind you as this will encourage an attacker. Instead, cross the road, glancing over your shoulder to check the traffic, and see if your follower does the same. If he does, go up to the nearest shop or 'safe' house (ie one with lights on and looks as though someone's home), explain your predicament and ask if you can telephone the police. Do this even if you are very close to your own home – you don't want a potential attacker to find out where you live.

If you are attacked, what should you do?

No one knows how they will react in such a situation until it happens. Some people freeze in fear, others fight back in their anger. What you'll do will depend on how you instinctively react in the first few seconds, but you should also take into account the situation itself.

If the attacker has a weapon, do as you are told – hand over your wallet, bag or whatever. If he hasn't, scream or yell as loudly as you can. Don't expect anyone to come to your aid (people don't like becoming 'involved') – but you might scare off an attacker who doesn't want to attract attention. If you have a rape alarm (there's no reason why men shouldn't carry one too), use it to disorientate the attacker for a few precious seconds and then run like hell to the nearest shop, brightly-lit house or busy street.

How can you protect yourself?

The legal position is that you can use 'reasonable' force to protect yourself or give yourself a chance to escape. You may well ask what 'reasonable' means, given you're the one in danger and you didn't ask to be attacked. Reasonable force means doing what's necessary to fend off your attacker and no more. In other words, if he has you pinned to the ground and your hand comes across a brick, you can use it to hit and stun the attacker and give yourself a few seconds to make your escape. You cannot keep on hitting him until he's senseless, however much you feel he deserves it. You could be the one who ends up being prosecuted.

You also run the risk of prosecution if you are caught carrying an offensive weapon, for example any sort of knife. Also mace canisters, which release a powerful chemical irritant and are a popular form of self-protection in the USA, are illegal in this country.

There is a more understandable objection to carrying a weapon for self defence: an attacker could take it off you and use it on you instead. If, however, you would feel safer carrying something with which you could protect yourself in an emergency, use something which you have a plausible reason for having on your person if you're stopped and questioned by the police. Your house keys, for instance, could be used to scratch and gouge an attacker's face. If you're a member of the college hockey or squash teams you could quite legitimately carry a hockey stick or racquet. Baseball bats aren't to be recommended as they are commonly used by muggers.

KEEPING YOUR HOME SAFE AND SECURE

Your home should be the one place you feel safe and unthreatened – and so you will, if you take a few sensible precautions.

If you live in a hall of residence

❑ Keep your door locked at night when you go to bed – and at any time during the day when you know most of the other students on your floor are out at college. When you come home late at night, make sure you lock the main front door – for everyone else's protection as well as yours.

❑ If you come across someone on the premises that you don't recognise, ask them who they are and why they're there. If you don't get a satisfactory answer, go to your hall's administrative office and report their presence.

If you live in a flat or lodgings

❑ Make sure all doors and windows are locked when you're out. Apart from the nastiness of having an intruder in your home and the loss and damage that can result, you could also find your insurance on your possessions is declared invalid if the intruder hasn't broken in, but entered through an open window or unlocked door.

❑ If you're not sure how secure you are, ask the crime prevention officer from your local police station to come and advise you. If your security really is inadequate, he/she may be able to encourage your landlord to make the necessary changes at his (rather than your) expense. Generally speaking, front doors should have a deadlock as well as a Yale lock (the latter can easily be opened), plus a bolt on the inside which the last person home at night should activate. Especially vulnerable areas are back doors, ground floor windows and any window that can be reached by climbing onto a wall or up a drainpipe.

❏ As soon as dusk falls, draw your curtains. This not only keeps the heat in, it keeps prying eyes out.

❏ When you come home, always make sure your keys are in your hand, ready to open the door. This minimises the time (especially at night) when you're vulnerable to possible attack. If possible, leave a light on in the hall so you can easily find the keyhole (and so you aren't going into a dark and empty house).

❏ If you live in a block of flats (or a large house divided up into flats) and you have your own doorbell at the main front door, use only your surname (not your first name or Ms/Miss) on the nameplate.

❏ If when you come home you think there is an intruder, don't go in and risk your own safety. Go to your nearest neighbour or public telephone and call 999 and ask for the police.

HOW TO DEAL WITH AN OBSCENE TELEPHONE CALL

Receiving a nuisance call is an unpleasant experience at best, and people tend to react in one of two ways. Some are shocked and upset, while others get angry and let fly with a volley of abuse down the line. Both reactions are understandable, but they play into the hand of the caller, who gets his kicks from upsetting his victims.

If you receive an obscene call (men, as well as women, receive them), keep your reaction calm and replace the receiver. If the telephone rings again, lift the receiver and listen but don't say anything. If it's the malicious caller again, quietly put down the receiver beside the telephone and leave it for a few minutes, before replacing it. The caller is likely to get bored very quickly if he doesn't get the expected response.

You should report an obscene call to the police – especially if the caller seems to know a lot about you or your movements. Both the police and British Telecom take nuisance calls seriously, and have ways of tracing them. If necessary, your telephone number can be changed and made ex-directory. BT also have a helpline on 0800-661441, which you can call during office hours.

Have your number registered ex-directory (so no one can get it from the operator) and be selective about who you give it to. If your telephone number is listed in the directory, use your initials rather than your first names or your marital status, so that someone going through the list at random can't identify your gender.

Don't answer the telephone with your name (ie 'Hello, this is John/Jane Jones speaking') or with your telephone number. Many malicious calls are made at random, rather than to a specific person. By using your name or telephone number when you answer you could fix yourself in the caller's memory and leave yourself open to further calls.

If the caller asks 'Who's that?' when you answer the telephone, insist they identify themselves first. They're calling you, not the other way round. If they refuse to say who they are, put down the receiver. Similarly, if they ask 'What number is this?', ask them what number they wanted, and then tell them whether or not they've got the correct number.

If somebody you don't know rings up and starts asking you personal questions about you or your home, do not give them any information. Companies sometimes 'cold call', especially in the evenings, which can be irritating rather than alarming. You can cut this type of call short with a polite 'I'm not interested thank you' and put down the receiver.

However, obscene phonecallers sometimes try to get their victims off guard and into conversation by starting with innocent-sounding questions before getting down to the heavy stuff.

Chapter 12

HELP!

Crucial things to know in an emergency when you have to act quickly

What to do if you are ill – when to call an ambulance – what to do if you have had unprotected sex – dealing with an emergency in the home – emergency first aid – fire – when you smell gas – what to do when the lights go out – wiring a plug and changing a fuse – unblocking a kitchen sink or toilet – your rights when dealing with the police – if you are burgled – what to do if you are stopped on your way home, arrested or have your home searched – if you have a complaint

One of the drawbacks of living on your own is that there isn't always someone else around to take charge in an emergency. Knowing what to do can save a lot of inconvenience – not to mention a whacking great plumber's fee when, for example, the kitchen sink gets blocked. There may even be a time when knowing what to do makes the difference between life and death – or at the very least, serious injury.

Everyone has minor mishaps from time to time. Serious illness, accidents or emergencies are mercifully rare. Should you ever find yourself in a situation where it's imperative (a) to know what action to take and (b) to do it quickly, this chapter provides a quick and practical reference.

WHAT TO DO IF YOU ARE ILL

If you need to see a doctor but your condition isn't too bad, the health centre will expect you to get yourself to the surgery. Telephone and make an appointment. If, as sometimes happens, you are told your doctor hasn't any appointments free that day, stress that you're not well and you really need to see someone as soon as possible. You will always be fitted in, however busy the surgery, although you may have to wait a while to be seen. If you are too ill to make it to the surgery, the doctor will come and see you. Try to telephone for an appointment as early in the day as possible, ideally before 10 am.

If you're taken ill during the evening, at night or over the weekend and you live in hall, get your nextdoor neighbour to contact the duty warden, who will call a doctor. If you live in a flat, call the surgery or get one of your flatmates to call for you. Out of surgery hours you'll hear a recorded message which will give another number to ring – this will be the doctor on call. Always state your name and address clearly, so the doctor doesn't waste time trying to find you.

CALLING FOR AN AMBULANCE

There are circumstances when expert emergency treatment may be necessary, in which case you should call for an ambulance. Dial 999, and the operator will ask you which service you want. Request an ambulance, giving clearly your name, address and telephone number, plus a brief description of the nature of the emergency.

You should call an ambulance when

- ❏ There's been an accident resulting in a major or uncontrollable loss of blood, a broken limb, a major cut, burn or laceration.

- ❏ Someone is in shock or has lost consciousness.

- ❏ Someone is suffering severe pain, constant vomiting or a severe allergic reaction.

- ❏ Someone has suffered an overdose of drugs, or drugs and alcohol combined (the attending paramedics will need to know what the drug is).

- ❏ A baby or small child in your care seems very ill and you don't know what's wrong (eg has a very high or a very low temperature, is extremely drowsy or is convulsing).

WHAT TO DO IF YOU HAVE HAD UNPROTECTED SEX

It happens sometimes. You have two options: (1) deal with the situation immediately and get a doctor or clinic to prescribe you the 'morning after' pill or (2) wait and see if you become pregnant, and then have an abortion (assuming that you don't want to be pregnant). The latter option has obvious implications, including the prospect of spending three weeks or more in an agony of suspense.

The morning after pill

This is a form of post-coital contraception which is only ever used in an emergency: after unprotected sexual intercourse, or to prevent pregnancy after rape.

The morning after pill is in fact a course of four pills, which contain approximately ten times the hormone dosage of an ordinary contraceptive pill. Because the dose is so high, there may be quite a lot of discomfort for the couple of days the pills take to act (nausea, cramps, heavy bleeding etc). The pills must be started as soon as possible – certainly within 72 hours of intercourse – and it's necessary to have a check-up afterwards to make sure they've been successful.

The morning after pill is available from a GP or family planning clinic, but out of surgery hours it may be quicker (speed is important) to contact your local branch of the British Pregnancy Advisory Service (BPAS) or Brook Advisory Centre (BAC). Both of these organisations are registered charities, and you'll find their telephone numbers and addresses in the telephone directory.

Having an abortion

If you become pregnant you will have to decide whether or not to continue with the pregnancy. While it's true that the sooner an abortion is carried out the better (the procedure is less complicated), it's very important that you allow yourself enough time to think your feelings through. You may find counselling very helpful, particularly in talking about the possible psychological consequences of having an abortion. You can talk to your doctor or your family planning clinic, or alternatively you can get help and advice from BPAS or BAC.

If you do decide to have an abortion you will need the consent of two doctors. Abortions are free on the NHS, but if there is likely to be a delay in getting an appointment you can have one more quickly in a private clinic (for which you will have to pay). Up to 12 weeks an abortion is performed by the suction method under local or general anaesthetic, and may (but not always) involve an overnight stay in a hospital or clinic. After 12 weeks the clinical procedures used are more complicated and therefore carried out under general anaesthetic, with an overnight stay in hospital.

Although an abortion solves the immediate problem of an unwanted pregnancy, it can take some time to get over the emotional effects and consequences. Again, counselling can be a great help.

DEALING WITH AN EMERGENCY IN YOUR HOME

Any hospital casualty and accident department will tell you that the home can be a dangerous place. Not a nice thought, when it's the one place you should feel happy and relaxed. However, the vast majority of accidents are preventable, with a few precautions and some common sense.

Once in a blue moon something may crop up that you need to know how to deal with immediately. Under your contract with your landlord he/she will be responsible for arranging repairs when, say, the roof suddenly develops a leak or the fridge or washing machine breaks down (unless they are your own personal property). But what do you do if the lights go out, you smell gas or the chip pan catches fire?

When an emergency happens you have to be able to keep a cool head and act quickly – and that means knowing exactly what to do and having important emergency numbers readily available by the telephone.

First aid kit

Keep a first aid kit where you can get to it quickly. You can buy a basic one from a high street chemist's shop, or make one up yourself. Fill a clearly labelled box or plastic container with the following:

- ☐ a packet of assorted size plasters for minor cuts etc
- ☐ sterilised absorbent dressings for placing over cuts and other injuries
- ☐ a crepe bandage for sprains or to hold dressings in place
- ☐ adhesive dressing strip and white gauze to secure dressings in place
- ☐ cotton wool for cleaning and wiping wounds
- ☐ a small pair of scissors
- ☐ safety pins
- ☐ a small bottle of antiseptic such as TCP
- ☐ some aspirin or paracetamol.

CUTS

The most important thing to do is stop the bleeding. If it's a minor cut or graze, the bleeding will stop fairly quickly once a dressing has been applied.

- ☐ Rinse the wound under a running tap to clean it.
- ☐ Dilute a little antiseptic according to the instructions on the label and very gently apply to the wound on a piece of cotton wool.
- ☐ Dry the wound and then apply a clean plaster.

More severe bleeding caused by a major cut needs quick action (so don't stop to clean it) and possibly professional treatment.

- ☐ Apply pressure to the wound by pinching the edges together until the bleeding stops (this can take up to 15 minutes). Raising the wound higher than the victim's heart helps slow the flow.

☐ Apply a thick pad over the wound, maintaining the pressure, and tie the pad securely in place with a handkerchief or belt.

Seek medical attention if:

☐ The bleeding hasn't stopped after 15 minutes.

☐ The wound has splinters, glass or dirt you can't remove easily. (A large piece of glass etc should be left in place for a paramedic or doctor to remove.)

☐ The wound is deep.

☐ The wound becomes infected or hasn't started to heal after a few days.

☐ You suspect something is broken.

BURNS AND SCALDS

A burnt finger or small scald should be held under a running cold tap for at least 10 minutes. (Cooling helps prevent further damage and relieves the pain.) Cover with a sterilised dressing and keep dry and covered until the blisters have healed. Never apply butter or antiseptic cream to a burn.

If the burn or scald is more severe, you'll need to apply first aid and then dial 999 for an ambulance.

☐ If clothing is burning, smother the fire with a blanket or large coat. (In the case of a scald, remove the soaked clothing.)

☐ Remove the burnt clothing but don't disturb any fibres that are stuck to the wound.

☐ The next important step is to cool the burned or scalded area. Immerse the burned area in a sink or bucket of cold water for at least 10 minutes. Alternatively, apply a thick pad soaked in cold water, dampening and cooling it as necessary until medical help arrives.

Seek medical attention if:

- ❏ The affected area is larger than the palm of a hand.
- ❏ The skin has been burned away.
- ❏ The face, hands or feet are affected.
- ❏ The burn doesn't seem to be healing within three days.
- ❏ There are other injuries.
- ❏ You have any worries at all.

FIRES

A few simple precautions could prevent most fires that occur in the home – and lessen the resulting injuries and deaths in the ones that do.

- ❏ Work out the best escape route in case of fire as soon as you move into your flat.
- ❏ Shut all doors when you go to bed to prevent the spread of smoke and flames if there's a fire in the night.
- ❏ Buy a smoke alarm if your flat hasn't already got one; you can get them for less than a fiver. Most of the deaths caused by fire are the result of smoke asphyxiation, and not flames. An alarm has a piercing shriek which will give you a precious few minutes' warning, enough time to make your escape.
- ❏ Buy a small fire extinguisher. Make sure you know exactly how to use it, should the need ever arise. A fire blanket is also very useful in putting out small kitchen fires like chip pan fires.
- ❏ Cigarettes are just about the most common cause of fire. Make sure they're properly stubbed out before emptying ashtrays into a wastebin. Don't smoke in bed – especially at night, when you could doze off and start the bedclothes smouldering. The smoke is likely to asphyxiate you before the flames can harm you.

❏ Switch off and unplug all electrical appliances (including the TV) at night before going to bed, and when not in use. Make sure, in particular, that an iron is switched off when not in use, and never leave it unattended. Do not overload sockets with adaptors; make sure plugs are correctly wired and that you use the correct fuse.

❏ If you have any doubts at all about the fire safety of your home, your local fire station will be happy to send an inspector around to check you out.

WHAT TO DO IF THERE IS A FIRE

❏ If it's a small fire, try to put it out using a fire extinguisher, or by smothering it with some heavy material such as a blanket, coat or rug.

❏ If the fire has taken hold or is obviously out of control, warn your flatmates and anybody else in the house and get to a place of safety. Do not stop to collect valuables. A fire spreads incredibly rapidly, and you may only have three or four minutes to get out. Once safe, call the Fire Brigade by dialling 999 and give your address clearly.

❏ If you suspect there's a fire in a room behind a closed door never open it to see. You'll let in more oxygen to fuel the flames and cause the fire to spread quicker throughout the flat. Call the Fire Brigade.

❏ If a frying or chip pan catches fire never try to put it out with water – you'll only make matters worse by spreading flames and hot fat everywhere. Also, do not attempt to pick up the pan and carry it outside. The flames could blow back in your face and if you drop the pan, the flames and fat will spread, possibly even over you. Switch off the source of heat and carefully place a heavy lid over the top of the pan, angling it in front of you rather than placing it straight down (otherwise the flames might leap up at you). If this doesn't work, get out of the kitchen closing the door behind you, and call the Fire Brigade.

OTHER DOMESTIC EMERGENCIES

IF YOU SMELL GAS

☐ DO NOT turn the light or other electrical switches on or off as the spark could cause the gas to explode.

☐ DO NOT smoke or use a naked flame.

☐ Open doors and windows to disperse the gas.

☐ Check if a gas tap on the cooker is on or a pilot light has gone out. If this isn't the source of the leak, turn off your whole supply at the meter. Call the gas board's 24 hour emergency number and tell them you have a leak; they'll send an engineer around immediately.

Precautions: Keep the emergency number by the telephone. Get your landlord to show you where your main gas supply tap is (it should be by the meter).

IF THE LIGHTS GO OUT

☐ Look out the window. If the street and neighbours' lights are out there's a general powercut in your area. There's nothing you can do until the electricity board has repaired the fault (they sometimes have a recorded message on their customer service telephone number estimating when this might be). Remember to turn off all lights and appliances – especially heaters, irons, electric ovens etc – if you go to bed or leave the flat before the powercut is over.

☐ If only you are affected, it could be that one of the wiring circuits that supply electricity to your flat's sockets and overhead lights has blown a fuse, either because of a sudden surge in power or because one of your appliances is faulty and its own safety fuse has failed to blow.

The first thing to do is to locate the main fuse box (also known as a consumer unit). Lift the lid and you'll see a row of individually labelled fuse cartridges, each of which relates to a specific circuit. The affected cartridge will have popped out. Turn off the main switch (so labelled) and push the cartridge back in. Turn on the main switch again; if nothing happens, you'll need to replace the cartridge fuse. If your landlord hasn't provided any spares, you'll need to get some from your local electricity showroom.

Many modern consumer units have a circuit breaker. Lift the circuit breaker's lid and you'll see a row of individually labelled switches or push buttons which, like fuse cartridges, relate to specific circuits. If your flat has one of these, look for the one that has tripped 'off' and switch/push it back on again.

If none of these actions helps something more serious is wrong and you must telephone your local electricity board. Remember that ELECTRICITY CAN KILL, so never tamper with the electrical system yourself.

Precautions: Keep some spare 60 watt (for side lamps) and 100 watt (for overhead lights) handy, plus some 3, 5 and 15 amp fuses. Make sure you know how to wire a plug accurately and change a fuse (see diagrams). Keep a torch and some candles and matches easily available in case of powercuts. Ask your landlord to show you where your flat's circuit breaker is.

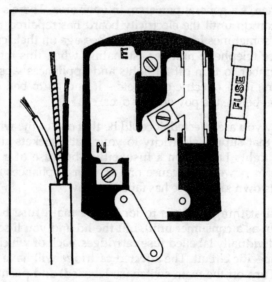

Wiring a plug: Stage 1

WIRING A PLUG AND CHANGING A FUSE

This couldn't be easier, but it's vital for safety reasons that it's done accurately. Plugs are usually sold with an accompanying diagram to show you what to do, otherwise take the back off another plug that's already wired up and use it as a guide. You'll need a small headed screwdriver and a sharp knife or scissors.

☐ Unscrew the plug cover. Unscrew and remove one of the flex clamp screws and loosen the other.

☐ Ease out the fuse with the tip of the screwdriver. Loosen the terminal screws so there's enough room to slip the wire in. Position the flex in the plug and then replace the flex clamp to keep it in place. Replace the flex screw, but don't tighten it too much.

☐ Manoeuvre the flex in the plug so that the three wires extend about half an inch beyond their designated terminals, which is as follows:

green and yellow wire to the Earth (marked E) terminal

blue wire to the Neutral (marked N) terminal

brown wire to the Live (marked L) terminal

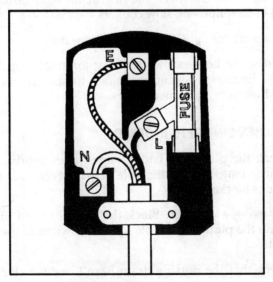

Wiring a plug: Stage 2

Strip away approximately a quarter of an inch of the insulation plastic covering each wire. Twist the strands of wire together and insert into its terminal hole and tighten the screw. This can be a bit fiddly.

❑ Replace the fuse.

❑ Check the wires are correctly positioned, then tighten the flex clamp screws and replace the back of the plug.

Choosing the correct fuse

A fuse is a safety device which stops the flow of electricity to an appliance when there's a sudden surge of power the appliance isn't designed to cope with. If it didn't do this, the appliance and/or its flex could dangerously overheat and cause a fire.

You must choose the correct size fuse for each individual appliance, and you'll find this marked or imprinted on the appliance and in the manufacturer's instructions.

3 amp fuses are for appliances up to 720 watts:

Radios; table lamps; TVs (although some manufacturers recommend a 5 amp fuse so check the instructions); electric blankets; audio and hi-fi equipment; slow cookers.

13 amp fuses are for appliances above 720 watts:

Irons; kettles; fan heaters; electric fires; toasters; deep fat fryers; fridges and freezers; washing machines; tumble dryers and spin dryers; dishwashers; vacuum cleaners.

IF THE KITCHEN SINK GETS BLOCKED

❑ Check the plug hole isn't clogged with debris. A simple drainer that fits over the hole helps prevent this and more serious blockages.

❑ Try using a plunger. Block the overflow and vigorously pump the plunger's handle up and down until the blockage shifts.

❑ Check that the outside drain hasn't become clogged with leaves.

❐ If the bath or bathroom sink is blocked see if the plug hole is bunged up with hair.

IF THE TOILET GETS BLOCKED

❐ You should be able to shift the blockage with a straightened metal coat-hanger or something similar. If this doesn't work, you will have to call a plumber (or get you landlord to).

YOUR RIGHTS WHEN DEALING WITH THE POLICE

In an ideal world you won't need to have contact with the police at all. But there may be occasions when you need their help – especially if you live in a rough area where there's a lot of crime. It's a good idea to keep your local police station's telephone number by the telephone in case you need to call it in an emergency. You can also call 999 and ask for police assistance – this can be quicker than trying to get through on your local station's number, especially if they're having a busy night.

IF YOUR HOME IS BURGLED

Always report it to the police. Your insurance company will usually require a *crime number* (which the police will give you) in order to settle your claim.

You should always call the police if you think an intruder is trying to get in, even if you manage to scare them off. An attempted break-in should always be taken seriously by the police. Sometimes it might be suggested to you that it's a prank, especially if it's known that you are a student. You have a right to insist that you are taken seriously, and that an officer is sent to investigate – especially as there may be a chance that the intruder is still in the area and could be picked up. If you or some of your flatmates are women, do mention this to the police (female students are accepted to be vulnerable in some university towns).

If you still feel that the police haven't co-operated adequately, speak to your college authorities (the college or student union welfare officer, the women's officer, your personal tutor). Also consider contacting your parents – an indignant and irate parent can work wonders!

WHAT TO DO IF YOU ARE STOPPED BY THE POLICE ON YOUR WAY HOME AT NIGHT

They may be on the look-out for someone whose description you superficially match. Be co-operative and answer questions as calmly and politely as possible. You'll be asked your name and address and what you're doing there at that time of night. DO NOT be cheeky or antagonistic. If the officer's attitude is provocative, don't rise to the bait – infuriating though it is when you know you're innocent. The officer may check your details over the radio and if you (a) haven't got a police record (b) have a plausible reason for your presence in the area and (c) aren't carrying anything likely to cause suspicion, you'll probably be let go there and then.

IF YOU ARE ARRESTED

Don't resist arrest, otherwise you could be charged with resisting arrest and obstructing a police officer in the execution of his/her duty. Don't discuss the situation with the officers on the way to the station, but wait until you've had a chance to speak to a solicitor. You may inadvertently and innocently say something damaging. Once at the station you will be allowed to contact a solicitor and then you can protest your innocence.

At the police station you will be informed of your rights which are:

- ❏ You can make a telephone call to let someone know where you are and that you have been arrested.

- ❏ You can consult a solicitor in private, on legal aid. If you don't have a solicitor you can ask to speak to the station's duty solicitor.

- ❏ You can consult the police codes of practice on detention, searches and identification parades.

The police have the right to search you if you have been arrested, and to remove personal items which will be returned to you on your release. Depending on the circumstances of your arrest you may be strip-searched, but only by an officer of the same sex. An 'intimate' search will only be carried out for drugs or weapons, and then only by a doctor or nurse, or under the authority of a senior police officer.

To protect you from being 'aggressively' interviewed, your interview with the police will be tape-recorded. You will be asked to give and sign a statement. All this should be in the presence of your solicitor.

IF YOU ARE CHARGED WITH AN OFFENCE

This means the police think they have enough evidence to connect you with the offence in question to go to court. You'll be formally cautioned that you don't have to say anything you don't want to, but that anything you do say may be taken down and used against you in court. You don't have to say anything without the presence of your solicitor. Depending on the type or severity of the charge, you will be released on bail or remanded in custody.

If the court clears you of the charge you may be able to sue the police for damages.

IF YOU ARE STOPPED ON SUSPICION OF DRINKING AND DRIVING

The police officer will ask you to take a breath test. Do not refuse. The legal limit for drivers (including bicyclists and motorcyclists) is 80 mg per 100 ml of blood. If the test is positive, you will be asked to go with the officer to the police station where you will undergo further tests (eg blood and urine) to confirm or otherwise the original results. If the results are positive you will be charged with drink-driving and release on bail, and will appear in court at a later date.

IF THE POLICE WANT TO SEARCH YOUR HOME

The police can enter and search your home if (a) you give them permission (b) they have a search warrant (c) they have reason to believe that someone is in physical danger.

A warrant is granted by a magistrate, who has to be satisfied that the police have good reason to search your home – eg they suspect you have drugs or stolen goods on the property, or that someone has committed an arrestable offence. You are entitled to examine the warrant, which should state the precise address to be searched and the items the police are authorised to search for and remove. You should also be given an itemised list of everything they subsequently take away with them.

You are legally entitled to refuse entry to the police if the details (eg the address) on the warrant are incorrect or if the police refuse to show you the warrant.

IF YOU FEEL YOU HAVE BEEN UNFAIRLY TREATED BY THE POLICE

You can make a complaint to the station's duty officer, or you can write to the Chief Constable of your local force, or to the Police Complaints Authority. Keep a written record of the events, including the identity numbers of the officer(s) involved and the names and addresses of any witnesses. If you are being held under arrest at the police station at the time you can request a pen and paper to make your own notes, and this should be granted.

Your complaint will be taken seriously and investigated, either informally (if it's a matter of getting an apology) or formally by a senior officer or the Police Complaints Authority. You may also be able to sue for damages. You can obtain legal advice from a Legal Aid solicitor, or from your local Citizens Advice Bureau or law centre.

INDEX

I think I'm developing an allergy to paper